Solomon and Cohen know media Bias and Blather like a rancher knows BS — and their latest book is an invaluable guide to help you shovel through the "news."

—**Jim Hightower**

If the adage for many investigative writers is "follow the money," Cohen and Solomon have taken a step forward by following both the money and the cameras. The result—a sharp, savvy media criticism that examines the ways the confluence of power in our society shapes the telling of so many stories to the detriment of the people. The term "media establishment" takes on new meaning through Cohen and Solomon's lens.

—**Julianne Malveaux**

Jeff Cohen and Norman Solomon do an outstanding job of contesting the fraudulent claim of the media's "liberal bias," demonstrating by numerous case studies the predominant command of conservatism. In story after story they show by example what an honest press serving a democratic function would have reported, but didn't.

—**Edward S. Herman**
coauthor, *Manufacturing Consent*

Two of the fiercest and most articulate media critics around.

—**Laurie Ouellette**
Utne Reader

Cohen and Solomon have solved the problem of "whose side are you on?" by being on the side of the reader, the viewer, the Joe or the Annie out there making an honest living fixing cars or grooming poodles while trying to make sense of the public debate in their spare time.

—**Molly Ivins**

D0089865

Through the Media Looking Glass

Decoding Bias and Blather in the News

Jeff Cohen

and

Norman Solomon

Common Courage Press   Monroe, Maine

Library of Congress Cataloging-in-Publication Data
Cohen, Jeff, 1951-
Through the media looking glass: decoding bias and blather
in the news
/Jeff Cohen and Norman Solomon.
p. cm.
Includes index.
ISBN 1-56751-049-3. -- ISBN 1-56751-048-5 (pbk.)
1. Journalism--Objectivity. 2. Mass media--Objectivity.
3. Journalism ethics. 4. Mass media--Moral and ethical
aspects.
I. Solomon, Norman, 1951-. II. Title.
PN4784.024C64 1995
302.23'0973'09045--dc20   95-10339
CIP

Common Courage Press
Box 702
Monroe, ME 04951

207-525-0900   fax: 207-525-3068

Second Printing

Contents

Part IX
Clinton Priorities on the Home Front

Part X
Scandals Hyped or Hidden

Part XI
Hidden History

Part XII
Human Rights Abroad

Foreword

A bit of wisdom from cowboys of yore: "Always drink upstream from the herd."

This is—and always has been—sound advice for swallowing journalism, too. The conventional media overwhelmingly impart the message of officialdom, of the economic powers, of the status quo...of the herd. Consume it at your own risk.

It's always been better to be upstream, drawing from pamphleteers like Thomas Paine, muckrakers like Ida Tarbell, iconoclasts like Izzy Stone and—today—freejournalists like Jeff Cohen and Norman Solomon.

Years ago, home for the holiday, I sat with my father watching a ballgame on television. An ad for a national chain of fast-food fish restaurants popped on the screen, blaring its tagline: "Our fish doesn't taste fishy!"

After a couple of blinks, Daddy turned to me and said, "Jim, I like my fish to taste fishy," realizing as he said it that The Powers That Be were not beyond tampering even with life's small pleasures.

So much of what passes for journalism today is a fast-food ad: "Our news doesn't taste like news!" Of course not. Instead, it's news "bits" whirred together, sanitized, colorized, "virtualized" and reconstituted—probably by the same global conglomerate that does the fish.

This is why so many Americans of such diverse and colorful political stripings hunger for the Cohens and Solomons: exuberant, yeasty, "unsanitized" journalists who are free of the conglomerate tethers that restrict news coverage to what is "fit to print."

I host *Hightower Radio,* a national talk-radio program that deals with many of the same "unfit" topics that Cohen and Solomon address in this book. The most common comment by callers to my program is that *these are the issues* they want to discuss—the issues of power, money and class that politicos, pundits and other pontificators pretend do not exist in America. The great majority of these folks are neither liberal nor conservative in any true ideological sense. The most important—and the most radical—political perspective in our country is not right to left...but top to bottom, and most Americans today realize they are no longer even in shouting distance of the economic and political powers at the top, whether those powers call themselves Republican or Democrat, Conservative or Liberal.

In column after column, and in plain language, Cohen and Solomon reveal that the central obstruction to our nation's democratic promise is this: Too few people control too much of the money and power, and they're using both to gain more of each for themselves...at your expense.

Now that's worth reading about. The truth might not set you free, but surely it'll get you moving in that direction.

Jim Hightower

Part I
Big Media, Big Money

The nation's dominant media companies keep getting larger in size and fewer in number. Meanwhile, leading journalists, TV anchors and pundits move even closer to America's economic and political elites. The more that wealth shapes the news business, the less we hear critical analysis of corporate power in our society.

Media Mergers: Good for Business, Bad for Democracy

"Too much power concentrated in too few hands is a threat to freedom."

This principle is one of the foundations of classical conservative philosophy. It's also a tenet articulated by liberals and progressives.

But today, with American media power merging into ever fewer hands, not many people are speaking out against this threat to freedom.

One man who's been sounding the alarm for over a decade is Ben Bagdikian, former journalism school dean and *Washington Post* editor. His 1983 book *The Media Monopoly* documented the negative impact of 50 corporations dominating the U.S. media.

Some saw Bagdikian as an alarmist when his book predicted that mergers would one day reduce the number of corporations controlling most of the media to a mere half-dozen. Nowadays, investment bankers on Wall Street make the same prediction.

At Bagdikian's last count, fewer than 20 corporations had majority control of the newspaper, magazine, book, TV and movie industries.

Bagdikian opposes the media concentration as "bad for democracy." Wall Street supports it as "good for business."

Recent merger developments have been so earth-shaking that even Congress stirred. [The Bell Atlantic phone giant announced it would merge with TCI, the country's largest cable TV company. But the deal later unraveled.]

Perhaps some in Congress are noticing that conglomerates often spout "free market" rhetoric to obscure their monopolistic practices. In the real world, oligopolies don't compete; they collude or merge—to the detriment of consumers.

It was once predicted that phone companies and cable

companies would aggressively compete in offering a variety of audio-video-computer services to each household: two-way television, hundreds of TV channels, access to libraries and college classes.

Instead of the expected slugfest between phone and cable firms, we're seeing a lovefest. When phone and cable companies marry, consumers lose choice. You take the service offered by your local monopoly, or you have no service.

With 1,200 local cable systems bringing TV into one out of five cable homes, TCI has become a mighty gatekeeper over programming. In the barely regulated realm of cable, TCI-Liberty Media chief John Malone has used his gatekeeper status to dominate the cable industry—to the point where he owns all or part of 25 national or regional cable channels, including Turner Broadcasting.

Organizations such as the Consumer Federation of America argue that control over both program content and the cable conduit should not be concentrated in the same hands. Look at Malone's history and you'll see why.

Malone and partners acquired The Learning Channel on the cheap. A suit charged that Malone had depressed the sales price by threatening to take the channel off his TCI cable systems.

Gatekeepers like TCI exercise life or death power over cable channels. Just ask CNBC—General Electric's cable network originally conceived as an all-news channel that would compete with CNN. After TCI acquired a major interest in Turner Broadcasting/CNN (and Malone joined Turner's board), CNBC could not gain entry to cable systems unless it abandoned plans to compete with CNN. It did so—becoming a financial and talk channel.

Who's to say the public wouldn't prefer competing all-news channels? The public didn't make the choice. The choice was made by John Malone, a political conservative who has expressed admiration for Rush Limbaugh.

If a powerful company like GE doesn't have the clout to fight through the gatekeepers, how likely would it be that a consumer channel launched by Ralph Nader or an environmental channel run by Greenpeace could ever get access?

Every year, a small number of corporations gain increasing control over cable TV—both conduit and content.

The advent of cable in the 1970s was heralded as the high-tech breakthrough that would transfer media power from a handful of broadcast companies to the public. It didn't.

Today, we're told that new technology will bring us a "superhighway" of information and entertainment through our phone line—and nearly limitless democratic choices. It won't.

The myth is that you can solve a political problem—media power concentrated in too few hands—by technological means. The reality is that political problems must be addressed through political means.

But few members of Congress have been willing to challenge the huge media firms that are determined to get even bigger.

[In December 1994, the ever-expanding TCI bought into "public" TV, acquiring two-thirds of MacNeil/Lehrer Productions.]

October 20, 1993

Decoding the Rich Pundits:
Who Do They Mean By "We"?

Journalists are supposed to expose secrets, not keep them. But when it comes to the salaries of national TV anchors and pundits, those secrets are well-guarded.

TV networks are mum on the subject—while news anchors claim to be in touch with average Americans, and pundits speak for "the middle class" and the necessity of "sacrifices."

Such pretensions might be hard to swallow if the public comprehended the enormous earnings of the talking heads. Some TV anchors get paid more in a few months than most of us earn in 40 years of work.

This month [February 1994] a bidding war broke out for Diane Sawyer. *The New Yorker* magazine says that Sawyer rejected ABC's salary offer of $4 million per year to keep her at that network, holding out for more than $8 million.

CBS offered her over $4 million annually to jump networks, and recruited its boardmember Henry Kissinger—a pal from when Sawyer worked for the Nixon White House—to help persuade her. NBC and Fox TV each made offers.

But when the smoke cleared, Sawyer had agreed to stay put at ABC—for a reported $7 million per year.

Multimillion-dollar raises in superstar salaries are part of a network trend of journalistic decline, staff layoffs and news bureau closings. That same money could pay for dozens of reporters, producers and researchers.

And what about the economic biases of the TV news stars? In theory, super-rich anchors and pundits might still be able to relate to poor or working-class Americans. In practice, they seem clueless about how most Americans live.

Sawyer, for example, has crusaded against "welfare cheats" who "gouge the taxpayers." One of Sawyer's cheaters was "Mary," a single mother with a four-year-old child who secretly worked two low-pay, part-time jobs to supplement her monthly welfare check of $600. Thanks to Mary's "fraud"— working off the books—her income totaled $16,700. "You know people say," Sawyer lectured her, "you shouldn't have children if you can't support them."

Or take the case of Patrick Buchanan, the TV pundit who ran for president as an "America First" populist—although campaign filings showed that the Mercedes-driving candidate made well over $800,000 in 1991.

Who is the "we" Buchanan spoke for recently when he proclaimed that "we have just begun to pay the biggest tax hike in history"? (Actually, other tax hikes have been bigger.)

If, by "we," Buchanan is referring to himself and others in the top 1 percent income bracket, he's not far from the truth. Families making more than $200,000 are paying 80 percent of the tax hike in the current budget.

If, on the other hand, Buchanan deploys "we" to refer to the broad American public, he's engaging in demagoguery. More than 98 percent of the public is not getting any income tax increase; working families earning less than $30,000 got their taxes cut.

It's not just Sawyer and Buchanan who are detached from the economic realities of average Americans. So are most TV anchors and pundits. And because of the elite bias of mass media discourse, basic economic facts are obscured.

Tax hikes on the wealthy are popular among the public, but not the pundits. In a 1992 speech, David Brinkley (estimated $1 million yearly income) attacked Bill Clinton's proposal to raise taxes on the rich as a "sick, stupid joke." Since there are so few wealthy, claimed Brinkley, such taxes "will soak the middle class." Rush Limbaugh (estimated $15 million) constantly makes the same charge. Ted Koppel (estimated $5 million) asserted on *Nightline* that high taxes on the wealthy in the 1970s "created a tremendous economic problem…. It didn't work."

FACT: Wealthy Americans are among the lowest taxed in the industrial world. From 1978 to 1992, tax cuts for the richest 1 percent of the population—average yearly income $567,000— added more than a trillion dollars to the national debt. In 1992 alone, these tax breaks cost the public $140 billion.

Cokie Roberts (estimated $700,000), George Will ($1.5 million) and other pundits encourage cuts in Social Security.

FACT: Social Security is the main sustenance of most elderly Americans; it's all that keeps a third of them out of poverty.

Pundits scapegoat labor unions and high wages for a lack of U.S. "competitiveness."

FACT: Real hourly wages have dropped 16 percent during the last 20 years. In 1973, U.S. manufacturing jobs were the highest compensated in the world; now a dozen countries have passed us.

Robert Novak (estimated $1 million) denounces proposals for universal health coverage as "socialized medicine," while Limbaugh denies there's a health care crisis in our country.

No crisis? Maybe Limbaugh is so rich he figures—in a pinch—he can simply buy himself a little hospital.

Whether conservative or centrist, whether residing inside the Beltway or in Manhattan, the millionaires of TV punditry are members of an elite, insular club.

The next time you hear one of them pontificating about what "we" must do to spur the economy or close the deficit, listen skeptically—and wrap your hands securely around your pocketbook.

February 16, 1994

Is "Media Ethics" Becoming an Oxymoron?

For years, comedian George Carlin has provoked laughs by pointing out oxymorons—seeming contradictions-in-terms such as *jumbo shrimp* and *guest host* and *military intelligence*.

Recent events suggest a new oxymoron: "media ethics." Only it's no laughing matter.

In theory, journalists are the public's watchdogs, shining a spotlight on the political and economic powers-that-be. But in practice, some of TV's leading news personalities have been taking their turns *in* the spotlight—as high-paid banquet and conference speakers for various economic interests.

In the Dec. 11 [1993] issue of *TV Guide*, reporter Marc Gunther exposed not only that industry lobby groups were lavishing big bucks on TV journalists, but that network TV executives didn't see much wrong with the practice. A CNN executive commented: "I'm proud when our guys can pick up a few extra bucks, and it's good exposure for CNN."

A few extra bucks? Not quite. TV news stars like Sam Donaldson and David Brinkley can earn $20,000 to $35,000 for a 40-minute speech.

"While viewers may not know it," Gunther reported, "the TV correspondent they rely on to explain health-care reform may have just pocketed a $5,000 lecture fee from a hospital group or insurance firm."

When ABC's *PrimeTime Live* deployed hidden cameras to expose ten Congressmen and their wives enjoying a free trip to Florida—paid for by an association of military contractors—the correspondent spoke critically of the "cozy relationship between public servants and special interests." But *PrimeTime's* co-host, Sam Donaldson, received $25,000 and first class treatment from the same lobbying group when he addressed its 1989 convention.

Where are the TV segments on the "cozy relationship"

between journalists and monied interests, and how it may affect reporting? Since 1991, members of Congress have been barred from accepting lecture fees. Not so for journalists.

The media analyst at ABC News is Jeff Greenfield. He says he won't speak to "partisan groups"—but he does give well-paid speeches to some of the most powerful media lobbies in Washington.

CBS medical reporter Bob Arnot has collected big fees for frequent speeches, including from associations of nursing homes and chain drug stores. He says he has turned down invitations from insurance or drug firms, including an offer of $37,000 for a single talk. One wonders what the drug company thought it would be buying.

Before becoming White House counselor to President Clinton last May, pundit David Gergen dispensed pro-corporate viewpoints on PBS's *MacNeil/Lehrer NewsHour*. Most of Gergen's income came from speeches—$700,000 from 171 talks in 16 months.

Cokie Roberts, who covers Washington for ABC and National Public Radio, makes more money in a few hours of speechifying—often to trade associations that lobby Congress—than most Americans earn all year.

Roberts says she would never adapt her views to suit a lecture sponsor. But she has things backwards. It's largely because of her corporate-friendly views that she is so sought after by business groups offering big honoraria. (Corporate interests don't offer such largess to critical commentators like Jim Hightower or Barbara Ehrenreich.)

If you need more evidence that "media ethics" is becoming an oxymoron, consider another recent disclosure: Turner Broadcasting System's $2,000 donation to the legal defense of Sen. Bob Packwood, a man covered regularly on CNN newscasts.

Turner's money helped Packwood retain one of Washington's priciest law firms in his defense against charges that he groped and sexually harassed two-dozen women. The senator, said a Turner spokesman, "is a friend of the cable industry"—one who has long opposed cable regulation.

News of the donation angered many journalists at CNN—who learned about it only because a CNN producer was exploring a possible feature on how corporations help politicians fight their legal battles. It's an important story—but the feature never materialized on CNN.

Finally, there is CBS's curious selection of Rita Braver as its White House correspondent. She was chosen in August, while her husband, Robert Barnett, was one of Bill Clinton's personal attorneys. During the campaign, Barnett prepped Clinton for the debates by playing the role of George Bush.

CBS proclaimed there was no problem in giving the White House beat to a reporter whose spouse was one of the president's current lawyers. Only after questions persisted in the press did Barnett say he would phase out his legal work for Clinton.

What does it say about TV journalism that CBS was unfazed by such an obvious conflict of interest?

It's the kind of media ethics question that news consumers might ponder over a helping of "jumbo shrimp."

[In July 1994, ABC News advised its correspondents not to accept major speaking fees from corporations and lobbying groups. The new policy immediately met with protests from Sam Donaldson, Cokie Roberts, David Brinkley, Brit Hume and others.]

December 8, 1993

Journalists Fail to Follow the Money in Washington

To learn how Washington works, you shouldn't have to go to the video store and rent a comedy. You should be able to rely on the news media.

But when it comes to understanding how special interests dominate Capitol Hill, you'll learn more by watching an Eddie Murphy farce than by watching TV news or pundit shows.

In "The Distinguished Gentleman"—about a con-man turned congressman—the Murphy character comes to Washington for the same reason Willie Sutton was attracted to banks: That's where the money is.

In one of the movie's illustrative scenes, a Washington lawyer-lobbyist sits down to lunch with the new congressman and explains that he's ready to raise money for the freshman no matter where he stands on the issues.

On sugar price supports: "If you're for 'em, I got money for you from my sugar producers in Louisiana and Hawaii. If you're against 'em, I got money for you from the candy manufacturers."

On limits for medical malpractice awards: "If you're for 'em, I got money from the doctors and insurance companies. If you're against 'em, I got money from the trial lawyers."

Dazzled, the newcomer to Congress asks: "With all this money coming in, how can anything ever get done?"

"It doesn't," responds the lobbyist. "That's the genius of the system."

This 90-second scene from a Hollywood movie sheds clearer light on Washington's business-as-usual than dozens of reports from national news outlets. That's because the Washington press corps defines news as what the politicians say and do— *not* how the monied interests and their lawyers pull the strings.

Take the case of Thomas Hale Boggs Jr.—known as

"Tommy" to the powers-that-be in Washington. He's well known to journalists…and a well-kept secret to most news consumers.

The dominant partner in his law firm (Patton, Boggs & Blow), Tommy Boggs appears to be the prototype for the lawyer in "The Distinguished Gentleman." Boggs and other superlobbyists have power over senators and members of the House because of all the money they steer to the politicians—through fundraising banquets and "bundled" contributions.

To get the attention of your congressperson, you might organize thousands of your neighbors to sign a petition. But Boggs gets the attention of your congressperson with something just as valuable: thousands of dollars in campaign donations.

Like Santa Claus in overdrive, Boggs bears gifts for Washington politicians not just on Christmas, but year-round. His law firm has a computer program that matches prospective corporate donors with members of Congress who need campaign funds; a match depends on what legislation is pending before a politician at any particular moment.

Once termed corruption or bribery, this kind of activity is legal in our high-tech era. That's partly because corporate lobbyists have a lot to say about "campaign finance reform." And because big news outlets too rarely scrutinize big money.

Boggs, whose parents were members of Congress, is a fierce opponent of spending limits and public financing of campaigns. Private financing serves him pretty well—his income is estimated at $1.5 million per year.

The Patton, Boggs firm boomed in the Reagan-Bush era, lobbying for almost every corporate interest under the sun: oil and gas, tobacco, pharmaceuticals, finance, insurance, Japanese-product importers, silicone breast implanters, Frank Lorenzo's Eastern Airlines, telecommunications, newspaper publishers, etc. The firm has also represented repressive governments such as Guatemala and Jean-Claude Duvalier's Haiti.

Patton, Boggs is expected to get even richer thanks to its close ties with the Clinton administration. Tommy Boggs was an early fundraiser for candidate Bill Clinton. And Ron Brown, former chair of the Democratic National Committee and now Clinton's secretary of commerce, was a partner in Boggs' firm for years.

As the debates about health care reform and NAFTA heat up, media coverage will intensify. Only in the margins will there be references to Tommy Boggs and his backroom brethren.

It's not that the Washington press corps is unfamiliar with the superlobbyists; Boggs' sister is Cokie Roberts—one of the superpundits. The problem is that establishment journalists don't question corporate dominance of national politics. Indeed, major news outlets are owned and sponsored by the same kinds of interests that Boggs is lobbying for.

Twenty years ago, two young journalists broke the Watergate scandal and brought down a deceitful president by heeding the advice: "Follow the money."

Today, the national press corps appears to be heeding a different maxim: "Ignore big money. It pays our bills too."

If journalists were doing their jobs properly, a light comedy starring Eddie Murphy wouldn't seem like such a revelation.

September 15, 1993

Just Imagine: A Media Crusade Against Big-Money Politics

After campaign finance reform died recently [fall 1994] in the U.S. Senate and health care reform was buried beneath the biggest avalanche of political donations in the history of Congress, we came across an astounding *Washington Post* column by Norman Ornstein, aka "Dr. Soundbite."

One of the most quoted experts in media history, Ornstein argued that campaign money "has a very limited impact" on Congress—and criticized the press for its "obsession" with the subject.

Ornstein's through-the-looking-glass view sparked a vivid fantasy, which we'd like to share with our readers. What if news media actually *were* "obsessed" with exposing the stranglehold that big money has on American politics?

In our fantasy, it's no half-hearted effort driven by an occasional news report or editorial. No, this media crusade roars from the web-fed presses to network TV.

It's the kind of crusade that media consumers have seen many times before—in the war on drugs or crime, or in the months before the Gulf War when many news outlets demonstrated a commitment to proving that Saddam Hussein was Adolf Hitler Jr.

Our fantasy is a media campaign that gets laws passed—like the "drug crisis" coverage that dominated the news a few years ago. The *New York Times* averaged close to three drug stories per day in 1988 and 1989, reaching a frenzy in September 1989 when the paper ran about seven articles each day on drugs.

Since journalists sustained that kind of coverage when illegal drug use was actually declining, imagine how much energy they could muster for tackling big money in politics—a problem that is getting dramatically worse.

All the ingredients exist for a story that causes news con-

THROUGH THE MEDIA LOOKING GLASS

sumers to be riveted—and angered. It names names, exposes politicians and their financial patrons "caught in the act," and reveals how the average voter has become a spectator in a "democracy" dominated by big campaign donors.

- Night after night, NBC's Tom Brokaw presents features on Washington "Greedlock," explaining—for example—how campaign donations from agribusiness firms derailed nutritional labeling on food products. We're shown which companies give the money, which members of Congress take it, and how the public is ripped off.

- ABC's Peter Jennings renames his "Person of the Week" segment "Person on the Take." He starts by featuring Rep. Jim Cooper (D-Tenn.), a once-obscure congressman who parlayed his pro-business "health care reform" proposal into a massive campaign war chest filled with money from insurance and drug company executives. And Jennings spotlights Sen. Ted Stevens (R-Alaska), who criticized a bill restricting lobbyist gifts to politicians by wailing: "You are going to close 90 percent of the restaurants in Washington."

- CBS's Dan Rather offers "They Bought the Ballot" segments. One assails the Philip Morris tobacco company for bankrolling the misnamed "Californians for Statewide Smoking Restrictions" whose initiative on the November '94 ballot would replace and *weaken* local smoking ordinances.

- ABC's 20/20 launches a regular "Greenwashing" feature, exposing such nice-sounding groups as "Oregon Citizens for Recycling" (formed by Union Carbide, Dow, Chevron, Exxon and Occidental Chemical) which spent $2 million to defeat a ballot measure offering genuine recycling.

- On Sunday politics shows, pundits begin scrutinizing the excessive money behind politics. Often cited as a symbol of the problem is lawyer-lobbyist Thomas H. Boggs.

Program host John McLaughlin gets into the spirit, bellowing angrily about the General Electric lobbyists who helped draft the corporate tax law that reduced the company's tax to below zero.

- *Meet the Press* devotes a whole program to the dealings of Dwayne Andreas, chair of the Archer Daniels Midland grain and ethanol company, which won favorable EPA rulings from President Bush after Andreas donated $400,000 in "soft money" to the Republican Party—and from the Clinton administration after he donated $100,000 to the Democrats.

- The media crusade regularly presents experts like Ellen Miller of the Center for Responsive Politics and Joan Claybrook of Public Citizen—detailing legislation that would solve the problem. Within months an aroused public is pressuring an exposed and intimidated Congress to pass serious reforms.

Wake up, folks! Time to return from Fantasyland. It's not going to happen that way—despite the recent debacles in Washington over health care and political reform.

Such a crusade would offend the powerful. And the biggest campaign donors are major media advertisers and owners who like the status quo.

Archer Daniels Midland sponsors *Meet the Press* and many weekend pundit shows, along with the *MacNeil/Lehrer NewsHour*; GE owns NBC and CNBC, and sponsors politics shows across the dial, including McLaughlin; CBS is owned by a tobacco tycoon; the executive producer of ABC's *20/20* is married to a major PR agent for the chemical and nuclear industries.

Which brings us to quotemaster Norman Ornstein, who has said he logged 1,294 calls from 183 news outlets in one year, a scholar who seems too busy appearing on TV to have much time for scholarship.

Ornstein works at the American Enterprise Institute, a think tank funded by the same monied interests that donate big bucks to politicians. He's the perfect "expert" for today's media: glib, credentialed, and propounding the view that mainstream media are overly "obsessed" with campaign funding. Unfortunately, he's no fantasy.

October 5, 1994

15 Questions About the "Liberal Media"

One of the most enduring myths about the mainstream news media is that they are "liberal." The myth flourishes to the extent that people don't ask pointed questions:

- If the news media are liberal, why have national dailies and newsweeklies regularly lauded those aspects of President Clinton's program that they view as "centrist" or "moderate," while questioning those viewed as liberal?

- If the news media are liberal, why is it that liberals are apt to be denigrated as ideologues, but status quo centrists or "moderates" are presented as free of ideological baggage?

- If the news media are liberal, why did most outlets praise Clinton's selection of David Gergen, who advocated Reagan policies, while pillorying civil rights lawyer Lani Guinier?

- If the news media are liberal, why did they applaud conservative White House appointees like Lloyd Bentsen and Les Aspin, while challenging liberals like Donna Shalala, Johnetta Cole and Roberta Achtenberg?

It also helps to look back at history and ask questions:

- If the news media are liberal, why have Clinton's meager tax hikes on the wealthy been referred to as "soaking the rich" or "class warfare," but President Reagan's giveaways to the wealthy were euphemized as "tax reform"?

- If the news media are liberal, why have national outlets been far tougher in scrutinizing Democratic presidents Carter and Clinton than Republicans Reagan and Bush?

- If the news media are liberal, why have they buried important facts, such as the shrinking of corporate income tax from 25 percent of federal expenditures in the 1960s to only about 8 percent today?

- If the news media are liberal, why have they given short shrift to reform proposals—tax-financed national health insurance, federally-supported child care, government jobs programs—that their own polls show are overwhelmingly popular with the public?

Pundits and commentators have gained increasing prominence in the media, often eclipsing the reporters:

- If the news media are liberal, why were the first two political pundits to appear on national TV every day of the week both conservatives: Patrick Buchanan and John McLaughlin? Was it their good looks?

- If the news media are liberal, why does the media spectrum typically extend from unabashed right-wingers to tepid centrists who go to great lengths—attacking progressive ideas and individuals—to prove they're not left-wing? Why do pundit debates on national TV have *Wall Street Journal* reporters representing "the left"?

- If the news media are liberal, why are TV pundit programs—even on "public television"—sponsored by conservative businesses like General Electric, Pepsico and Archer Daniels Midland?

- If the news media are liberal, why was Rush Limbaugh the first host in the history of American television to be allowed to use his national politics show to campaign day after day for a presidential candidate?

- If the news media are liberal, why do right-wing hosts usually dominate talk radio—even in liberal cities?

- If the news media are liberal, why are there dozens of widely syndicated columnists who champion corporate interests, but few who champion consumer or labor rights?

In analyzing the bias of any institution, it helps to look at who owns it. Which leads to a final question:

- If the news media are liberal, why are they owned and sponsored by big corporations that spend millions of dollars to lobby *against* liberal measures in Washington?

June 9, 1993

Part II
The Public's Airwaves?

Broadcasting began with high hopes in this country. But the federal government soon established itself as a protector of corporate control of the airwaves. Today, even "public" radio and TV are enmeshed with the same powers that dominate avowedly commercial stations.

Fate of Broadcasting Virtually Sealed 60 Years Ago

If you turn on a radio and sample dozens of stations, you may not think much of what's on the air. The commercialism and lack of diversity are apt to seem normal. But it didn't have to be this way.

Sixty years ago, in May 1934, a hard-fought battle reached the floor of the U.S. Senate. Lawmakers debated the future of broadcasting. The result was the landmark federal Communications Act.

Today we take it for granted that the finite space on the radio dial is dominated by large corporations. Even on "public radio," where the sponsors are called "underwriters," big bucks largely determine what will be heard.

But when radio was very young, few people assumed that "the ether" should be turned over to companies pursuing private profit. As late as 1928, even the interim Federal Radio Commission acknowledged that "advertising is usually offensive to the listening public."

That commission routinely sided with CBS, NBC and other new radio giants—while cutting the hours and watts of nonprofit stations run by colleges, labor unions, religious groups and civic organizations. Those nonprofit broadcasters were some of radio's pioneers.

As the feds "reallocated" radio frequencies, the nonprofit stations steadily lost out to the "chain stations." By 1931, over 90 percent of the stations broadcasting at 5,000 watts or more were affiliated with a national commercial network.

Some big stations—such as WGN, owned by the *Chicago Tribune*—got "clear channel" licenses to broadcast at 50,000 watts. And, as corporations grabbed the airwaves, annual revenues from radio advertising soared—from peanuts in 1927 to $100 million in 1930.

"Never in our history has there been such a bold and brazen attempt to seize control of the means of communication and to dominate public opinion as is now going on in the field of radio broadcasting," said the director of a station operated by the Chicago Federation of Labor.

Also battling the radio trusts was a small order of Catholic priests, the Paulist Fathers, based in New York. Their station, WLWL, often provided working-class listeners with discussions of social issues. Federal authorities squeezed WLWL's broadcast hours, contending it was a "special interest" station.

That infuriated the Rev. John B. Harney, who fired back that WLWL was "not a special interest, unless you want to say that those who are working for public welfare are pursuing special interests and that the gentlemen who are working for their own pockets are not."

Resentment toward audio hucksters was widespread. Blaring commercials were new—and jarring. In 1932, *Business Week* magazine declared: "Radio broadcasting is threatened with a revolt of listeners…. Newspaper radio editors report more and more letters of protest against irritating sales ballyhoo."

Two years later, renowned educator John Dewey warned: "The radio is the most powerful instrument of social education the world has ever seen. It can be used to distort facts and to mislead the public mind." He continued: "Whether it is to be employed for this end or for the social public interest is one of the most crucial problems of the present."

Activists built a radio reform movement, with petitions and newsletters and lobbying drives, to resist the broadcast monopolies. But most print media were unsympathetic.

The scant coverage that the press devoted to the radio reform battle was usually slanted in favor of the broadcasting companies. By the early 1930s, many newspapers had gained major holdings in profitable radio stations.

And quiet deals were cut in high government places. One factor: Many politicians, from President Franklin Roosevelt on down, were dependent on radio networks to carry their speeches.

Drew Pearson and Robert S. Allen got it right in their "Washington Merry Go-Round" column on Nov. 30, 1933: "A secret move is on foot to perpetuate the present monopoly which the big broadcasting companies have on the choice wavelengths."

Aided by the Roosevelt administration and allies on Capitol Hill, corporate broadcasters were able to usher in the Federal Communications Commission—still in existence today—established by the Communications Act of 1934.

Just before the Act's passage, the *New York Times* ran the headline "New Communications Bill is Aimed at Curbing Monopoly in Radio." The truth was just the opposite.

The Act stands as a monument to corporate power in U.S. broadcasting—and as a tombstone for democratic use of the airwaves.

In a last-ditch effort to head off radio monopolization, a grassroots campaign sparked by church and labor activists lobbied to set aside 25 percent of radio frequencies for nonprofit broadcasters. The measure was known as the Wagner-Hatfield amendment.

Commercial broadcasters fought back fiercely, and successfully. The Wagner-Hatfield amendment lost, 42-23, in the Senate. This defeat of public-interest forces in 1934 set the stage for private-interest control of American television later on.

All of this hidden history is excavated by scholar Robert W. McChesney in his meticulous new book, *Telecommunications, Mass Media, and Democracy.*

The radio reform movement was thwarted by the great extent of corporate media control that already existed. As McChesney notes, "The network-dominated, advertising-supported basis of U.S. broadcasting was anything but the product of an informed public debate."

After 1934, he points out, "Congress would never again consider fundamental structural questions in its communications deliberations. The legitimacy of network-dominated, advertising-supported broadcasting was now off-limits as a topic of congressional scrutiny."

Today's Congress remains uninterested in questioning corporate control of the airwaves that are supposed to belong to us all.

May 4, 1994

Who's Heard, and Who Isn't, on Public Airwaves

This is a column about who gets to speak—and who doesn't—on our country's "public" airwaves.

With the health reform debate heating up, you might think National Public Radio is a good place to hear analysts offering a variety of views. After all, NPR is not heavily sponsored by drug companies, insurance firms or other special interests with a direct stake in the debate.

What NPR doesn't tell you is that both of its congressional pundits on *Morning Edition*—former Democratic Rep. Tom Downey and former Republican Rep. Vin Weber—are paid political operatives for private health interests.

Downey and Weber are supposed to offer contrasting views. But on health care, they're both paid by the same side—the side that wants to prevent serious reform.

Downey is a lobbyist for Metropolitan Life Insurance and a division of Merck pharmaceuticals; he has also represented the U.S. Healthcare Inc. health maintenance organization. Big insurers and HMOs will benefit from "managed competition" proposals—like those of President Clinton or Rep. Jim Cooper—that keep health care in the hands of a shrinking number of giant corporations.

Weber is a political consultant for the United Healthcare HMO—as well as the Alliance for Managed Competition, a powerful coalition of the "Big Five" health insurance companies that includes Metropolitan Life.

Met Life executives never have to worry that a Downey-Weber "debate" on health care will question why giant firms like theirs take precedence in Washington over the public. In a sense, both "debaters" are on their payroll.

And there's no need to worry that either of NPR's congressional analysts will speak kindly of the "single-payer" proposal, which would eliminate private insurance firms (along with much waste and profiteering) from health care. According to the Congressional Budget Office, single-payer would cut costs while providing full, choice-oriented universal coverage.

But in three Downey-Weber discussions on health care since September 1993, single-payer has not been a serious option; Democrat Downey once referred to its 90 congressional backers as "the far left."

For many months, *Morning Edition* simply introduced Downey and Weber as "former congressmen." These days, they're also identified as "lobbyists." But *who* they lobby for remains hidden from listeners.

If NPR were airing the views of two lawyers who represented clients with interests relevant to the debate, those clients would be identified up front. But political pundits who represent corporate clients are granted virtual secrecy.

Asked why the clients of Downey and Weber are not identified on the air, *Morning Edition* senior editor Ellen McDonnell responded: "Do you think our audience is so naive that they think people trained in a specific line of work are now out there making pizza?"

Downey and Weber brought their "training" to a May 12 [1994] discussion of bills barring Congress members from receiving gifts from lobbyists. NPR's pundit-lobbyists went on at length—in tandem—deriding the bans as "massive silliness." Congress, declared Weber, "is so much freer of corrupt influence than it was 20 or 30 years ago."

As Washington's *Legal Times* reported in March, Downey and Weber are hardly alone as pundit-lobbyists. Televised pundits like Democrat Bob Beckel of *CBS This Morning* and Republican John Sununu of CNN's *Crossfire* work for various corporate clients—although that's not acknowledged to viewers.

If you've ever wondered why national pundit programs do such an abysmal job of examining corporate influence on politics, one factor is that many pundits themselves are on the gravy train. Another factor is that large companies sponsor the broadcasts.

In theory at least, National "Public" Radio is not dominated by corporate sponsors—and should be free to look beyond the Downeys and Webers and other insiders for independent commentators and analysts.

Yet a four-month study in 1991 conducted by FAIR (the media watch group we're associated with) showed no more diversity among NPR's experts than on the commercial networks. Of 27 commentators featured at least twice on *Morning Edition* or *All Things Considered*, for example, only one was not white and only four were female.

A couple of weeks ago, *All Things Considered* was set to make the kind of bold departure from all the usual suspects that one would hope for from public broadcasting. Death row inmate and black activist Mumia Abu-Jamal was to begin a series of commentaries about crime and prison life.

From 1979 to 1981, Abu-Jamal was a respected radio journalist in Philadelphia at an NPR affiliate and commercial stations. But his life took an abrupt turn in December 1981, after an altercation with a policeman left the officer dead; Abu-Jamal was sentenced to death as a murderer.

In the dozen years since, an international movement has formed—including the NAACP Legal Defense Fund—seeking a new trial for Abu-Jamal.

In his recorded commentaries for NPR, however, Abu-Jamal was not discussing his own case. He was to offer listeners a feeling for life behind bars from his unique perch; not many experienced broadcasters sit on death row.

But the day before this experiment in radio commentary was to begin, NPR's top management folded—under pressure from police organizations—and canceled the series. (Pacifica Radio, a much smaller network, is now planning to air his commentaries.)

Why such fear over some commentaries from death row? The real threat to society is that—instead of authentic debate on our country's pressing problems—we're bombarded by a narrow range of pundits representing private interests that aren't even identified.

[Downey and Weber continued as *Morning Edition* congressional analysts after their June 1994 appointments as bipartisan co-chairs of the Alliance for GATT Now, a coalition of business groups lobbying for passage of the trade pact.]

May 25, 1994

New Study Exposes Senate Blather on Public TV

Some politicians love to denounce public television as a bastion of anti-establishment bias. But a new study of public TV, released in August [1993], shows the absurdity—and inaccuracy—of much of the standard political rhetoric.

Last year, Senate Republican leader Robert Dole attacked what he called public TV's "unrelenting liberal cheerleading." He charged that "broadcasting apologists are hiding behind Big Bird, Mr. Rogers and *Masterpiece Theatre*, laying down their quality smokescreen while they shovel out funding for gay and lesbian shows."

Other conservative senators targeted specific documentaries. Sen. John McCain (R-Ariz.) criticized "Maria's Story," which favorably depicted a Salvadoran peasant who joined the guerrilla movement. Sen. Jesse Helms (R-N.C.) crusaded against "Tongues Untied," a film exploring the lives of African-American gay males—a minority within a minority.

To hear these senators tell it, public TV regularly "shovels out" programming for and about gays, guerrillas and rabble-rousers.

Are the claims true? Not according to the new study—the first ever to take a serious look at the full schedule aired on PBS stations across the country. It scrutinized the evening lineup for six randomly selected weeks spanning the first half of 1992.

The study focused on who gets to speak—in studio or on tape—on public affairs shows, analyzing 1,644 sources or "experts" appearing on 114 separate programs.

How many of the 1,644 sources were gay or lesbian advocates? Zero.

How many were leftist guerrillas? Zero.

Did progressive activists dominate public television? Hardly. Representatives of racial or ethnic groups accounted for a mere 1.6 percent of total sources. Labor union representatives were 0.9 percent of the total, environmental advocates 0.6 percent, and feminist spokespersons 0.2 percent.

Certainly a network accused by Sen. Dole of "unrelenting liberal cheerleading" must feature more Democrats than Republicans? Wrong again. During the period studied, both major parties were well-represented, but Republican sources outnumbered Democrats 53 to 43 percent. The rest were mostly Perot backers.

So who dominates the public affairs programs on PBS? Mainly we hear from government officials (23 percent of all sources), corporate representatives (19 percent), journalists from generally mainstream publications (12 percent) and academics from establishment or conservative institutions (6 percent).

Given the data, how did the vocal Senate critics of public television get it so wrong? The problem is that they responded more like censors than scholars, seizing upon particular programs that offended them.

For example, instead of recognizing that plenty of conservative foreign policy analysts regularly appear on PBS shows to balance the one documentary sympathetic to a Salvadoran guerrilla, Sen. McCain teed off on that one documentary.

The academics who conducted the public TV study—sociologist David Croteau, Vassar College professor William Hoynes and Fulbright scholar Kevin Carragee—didn't make the error of "anecdotalism." Analyzing the national evening lineup as a whole, they found that public affairs documentaries make up only 8 percent of the schedule—and that these occasional programs, so vilified on Capitol Hill, "are not characterized by a consistent liberal bias."

Documentaries comprise about one-third of the public affairs lineup—which is made up mostly of news, business and political talk shows. These daily and weekly programs—which include the *MacNeil/Lehrer NewsHour*, *Nightly Business Report*, *Wall $treet Week*, *Adam Smith's Moneyworld*, Bill Buckley's *Firing Line*, John McLaughlin's two shows, and *Washington Week In Review*—run the spectrum from establishment center to the right.

Perhaps more important than the right-left spectrum is the

top-down spectrum. The powerful voices of corporate and political elites are booming on public TV, while citizen activists are barely audible—just like in commercial broadcasting. In this regard, public TV has failed miserably in fulfilling its original mandate to "provide a voice for groups in the community that may otherwise be unheard."

The new public TV study—endorsed by an array of consumer, civil rights and public interest groups—is being distributed to public TV programmers across the country.

But there's another group that should take the time to read it: Senators who presume to judge a whole TV network based on a few documentaries they dislike.

August 18, 1993

Part III
Talk Radio

They've become media icons and potentates— savvy insiders who claim to be outsiders—talk show hosts with crafty deliveries and very conservative agendas. Via national syndication, and in city after city, they fill millions of radios with pseudo-populist appeals, misinformation and hate.

Advice to Rush Limbaugh:
Plead Temporary Insanity

This column is a public service offered free to someone who is in desperate need of help.

Our aim is to rescue Rush Limbaugh, a man whose words are venerated by millions of followers listening to him on more than 600 radio and 200 TV stations.

Limbaugh needs help. No one in the history of American broadcasting has been handed such awesome political power. Day after day, his monologues go unchallenged by any opposing views, facts or figures.

Listen to how he cried out for help on his radio show in August [1993]: "I do not make things up for the advancement of my cause. And if I find that I have been mistaken or am in error, then I proclaim it at the beginning of a program or as loudly as I can."

Given his huge following, Limbaugh knows he has a responsibility to correct the record. And since he makes so many errors—indeed, he demonstrates a compulsion toward disinformation—and corrects so few, we've volunteered to give him the help he's been begging for.

Begin by retracting some wild comments that even you—in your private moments, away from an audience—know are not true.

- "Most Canadian physicians" come to the U.S. when they are in need of surgery.

- "There is no conclusive proof that nicotine's addictive and the same thing with cigarettes causing emphysema, lung cancer, heart disease."

- "Women were doing quite well in this country before feminism came along." (*Before feminism* women couldn't even vote.)

Then correct the following false claims by offering the true figures—which we've included here to make it easy for you.

- "The poorest people in America are better off than the mainstream families of Europe." True figures: The yearly income of the poorest 20 percent of Americans is $5,226, while the average income in Germany, France, Britain and Italy is $19,708.

- "Budget figures show that actual construction of public housing *increased* during the Reagan years." Actually, in 1980, some 20,900 low-income public housing units were under construction; in 1988, there were 9,700, a decline of 54 percent. In that period, the new construction budget was slashed from $3.7 billion to $573 million.

- "Not one indictment" resulted from Lawrence Walsh's Iran-Contra investigation. In fact there were 14 indictments—most of which resulted in convictions or guilty pleas.

Next, correct the following distortions by clarifying who your sources are.

- When you repeatedly claim that volcanic eruptions do more harm to the ozone layer than human-produced chemicals, tell the public that your source on the volcano theory is a magazine produced by the wacked-out Lyndon LaRouche network—and that atmospheric scientists long ago rejected that theory.

- When you declared that the Clintons send their daughter to a school which "required students to write a paper on 'Why I Feel Guilty Being White,'" you went on to add: "My source for this story is CBS News. I am not making it up!" You should inform your audience that CBS News never reported the false story—and that your actual source was *Playboy*.

Now, admit that sometimes you get so emotional about advancing your cause that you can't keep yourself from overstatement or invective.

- In May [1994], there was your TV tirade against former NBC News president Michael Gartner after he wrote a column criticizing the recently deceased Richard Nixon. You accused Gartner of having "years and years of experience faking events"—and that he aired faked news "with the express hope of destroying General Motors."

- On your March 10 [1994] radio show, you spoke in urgent tones of "news" that a newsletter claimed "Vince Foster was murdered in an apartment owned by Hillary Clinton." The newsletter mentioned neither murder nor Hillary Clinton's apartment; on a later Ted Koppel ABC special, you deftly dissembled: "Never have I suggested that this was murder."

Finally, agree to seek further guidance for your problem. The above falsehoods from your books and broadcasts are a few of the dozens on topics from Whitewater to AIDS to taxes that are compiled in a report released this week: "Rush Limbaugh's Reign of Error." Study the report—published by our associates in the media watch group FAIR—and fill up the next few weeks of broadcasts correcting the record. That way, during those weeks, you won't have to worry about making any new errors.

Now, dear reader: You're probably wondering what *you* can do to aid this man in need. One way might be to send this column to your local Limbaugh TV or radio outlet—and suggest to the station managers that they can help Limbaugh help himself by remembering that old broadcasting concept of conflicting viewpoints.

If Limbaugh engaged in genuine debates, an opposing voice would be present to correct the record as soon as Limbaugh opened his mouth—or closed it, if such were possible—and there'd be no need for voluminous special reports listing his fallacies.

Here's a final piece of advice for Limbaugh: Beat the charges of distortion and falsification by pleading "temporary insanity." Acknowledge that whenever you are in front of a mike or an audience, you lose all responsibility for your actions...and your words.

June 29, 1994

ACCORDING TO NASA SCIENTISTS, THE OZONE LAYER REACHED RECORD LEVELS OF DEPLETION THIS SUMMER...YOU PROBABLY DIDN'T HEAR ABOUT IT THOUGH, SINCE NASA--FEARFUL OF A POLITICAL BACKLASH FROM RIGHT-WING ACTIVISTS--CHOSE TO *DOWNPLAY* THE INFORMATION...

APPARENTLY THESE ACTIVISTS WOULD RATHER RISK THE HEALTH OF EVERY LIVING BEING ON THE PLANET THAN ADMIT THE *POSSIBILITY* OF A PROBLEM...RUSH LIMBAUGH LEADS THE CHARGE, VOCIFEROUSLY DENYING THE VERY *EXISTENCE* OF A HOLE IN THE OZONE...

TOM TOMORROW © 9-21-93

A Dud for the Dittoheads:
Limbaugh's Empty Response

For someone claiming to be the "truth detector" who is "serving humanity" with "talent on loan from God," Rush Limbaugh has served up a major disappointment.

Over the last three months, his millions of devoted followers—the "dittoheads"—have been stranded in talkshow limbo. They've been waiting for the cult leader of the airwaves to release his long-promised "point-by-point rebuttal" to an early summer [1994] report documenting "Rush Limbaugh's Reign of Error." That report was issued by FAIR, the media watch group with which we're associated.

On Oct. 11, Limbaugh's "rebuttal" finally arrived—not with a bang but a dud. Limbaugh's 37-page manuscript was so empty of documentation that it provoked a skeptical news article in the *Washington Times*—one of the most stridently conservative dailies in the country. A livid Limbaugh assailed the *Washington Times* reporter on his radio show, and called the reporting "laughable."

Unfortunately, dear dittoheads, you can't blame the *Washington Times*. After laboring mightily for months, your holy man has brought forth a mouse of a document—neither a "rebuttal" nor "point by point." It only offers a defense of about half of the original 43 false or foolish claims, and the responses amount to obvious evasions and endless "what I was really saying" digressions.

Limbaugh admits to just a few of his scores of errors. (For instance, he concedes misattributing a religious quote to James Madison.) But his main approach is: Since I don't have the facts on my side, I'll hide behind a blizzard of words.

For example:

- Implying a media cover-up of Whitewater, Limbaugh said in February [1994]: "I don't think the *New York Times* has run a story on [Whitewater] yet....there has not been a big one, front-page story about this one that we can recall." The self-styled Whitewater expert couldn't recall that the *New York Times* broke the story in March 1992 on its front page.

His "rebuttal" complains: "The fact that I over-looked one *Times* article that ran 11 months earlier is hardly indicative of a 'reign of error.'" So now, still more errors rain. He'd overlooked not one but a half-dozen front-page *Times* stories on Whitewater; the first had run 23 months earlier, not 11.

- Limbaugh had proclaimed that "banks take risks in issu-ing student loans and they are entitled to the profits." In fact since the federal government guarantees defaulted student loans, they are risk-free.

  In a half-hearted defense of his foolish comment, Limbaugh quotes a banking official who says the "risk" is that the government won't reimburse banks if they don't follow proper procedures.

- Limbaugh had declared on radio that "the videotape of the Rodney King beating played absolutely no role in the con-viction of two of the four officers." Yet the jury foreman in the case had already stated that the video was "crucial" in the convictions.

  Limbaugh's assertion that the video played no role in the verdict, he now says, was "in the realm of opinion." Nothing in his meandering couple of pages refutes the jury foreman.

- The talkshow host had asserted that "there was not one indictment" in Lawrence Walsh's Iran-Contra probe. In fact, 14 men were indicted—including Oliver North, who went on to become a substitute host on Limbaugh's radio show.

  In "rebuttal," Limbaugh writes: "I obviously mis-spoke when I said there were no indictments—I clearly meant to say there were no *convictions,* a point I have made on many occasions." Then he writes of "no convictions on the substantive points." *Huh?* Most of the 14 indictments resulted in convictions or guilty pleas, many of them felonies.

- Limbaugh had claimed that "we have more acreage of forest land in the United States today than we did at the time the Constitution was written." Not so, says the U.S. Forest Service.

  The best Limbaugh can do in defending his error is to offer a quote from a book, which favorably compares U.S. forest land today with that in 1920. An alert reader will remember that the Constitution was written in 1787, not 1920.

- "There are more American Indians alive today than there were when Columbus arrived or at any other time in history," proclaimed Limbaugh. Not true, says the U.S. Bureau of Indian Affairs.

  Limbaugh's response: Since he can't find a source to support his claim, he quotes an academic, writing in the Heritage Foundation magazine, who says only that "some Indian groups are more populous today than in 1492."

- On his TV show, Limbaugh accused former NBC News President Michael Gartner of faking news "with the express hope of destroying General Motors."

  After three months of waiting, what proof does Limbaugh produce? Absolutely nothing.

- Straddling the border between the merely inaccurate and the bizarre, Limbaugh had declared on TV that Anita Hill "wanted to continue to date" Clarence Thomas. Dittoheads and laypersons alike eagerly awaited the blockbuster evidence, since neither Hill nor Thomas had ever described dating each other.

  Limbaugh now writes: "My comment about Hill dating Thomas actually demonstrates my recall of the Thomas-Hill episode." And then he offers a lengthy quote from a Hill-bashing book that doesn't mention dating at all.

- In his second book, Limbaugh wrote that "most Canadian physicians who are themselves in need of surgery, for example, scurry across the border to get it done right: the American way."

   Wading through three pages of "rebuttal" text, no evidence whatsoever is offered of Canadian doctors seeking surgery in the U.S.—although there is evidence of Canadian doctors seeking *work* in the United States. He solves the problem by passing off his serious book passage as "an obvious humorous exaggeration."

Rush Limbaugh would be comical if not for his dead serious devotees, many of whom are willing to believe his absurd statements—even the ones that are self-contradictory.

When Limbaugh dissects the doubletalk of Bill Clinton, he exhorts his followers: "Words mean things." It's one of Limbaugh's "35 Undeniable Truths of Life."

But when it comes to his own claims, Limbaugh sounds more like Humpty Dumpty in Lewis Carroll's *Through the Looking Glass*: "When *I* use a word, it means just what I choose it to mean—neither more nor less." Speaking of Humpty Dumpty, didn't he have a great fall?

October 12, 1994

Why Are Blacks the Media's Most Infamous Bigots

You can't see the news these days without encountering lengthy reports on the hateful pronouncements coming from a few black extremists.

The anti-white, anti-Jewish demagoguery of Nation of Islam leaders was recently examined, for example, in a 12-page *Time* magazine cover spread, and in two ABC *Nightline* episodes—one titled "Confronting Black Racism."

A central question running through such reports is whether black politicians and civic leaders have sufficiently denounced the mean-spirited rhetoric.

Given all the news coverage, you might think black prejudice against Jews and whites has become the dominant bigotry in our country.

Think again. Old-fashioned white racism is alive and kicking. But somehow, it doesn't arouse the same outrage in the national media.

By now, almost everyone has heard of Khalid Abdul Muhammad, the Nation of Islam speaker who spouted anti-white hate to a college audience of hundreds—and was denounced for weeks in the media and in a resolution that passed the U.S. Senate, 97-0.

But how many have heard of Bob Grant? Week after week, he spouts anti-black hate to much larger audiences—hundreds of thousands. He hosts the biggest show on the biggest talk radio station in the country, New York's WABC.

If you aren't familiar with Grant, that's not your fault—it's the national media's.

New York is the media capital of the country. But few journalists have voiced outrage over a talk show host who routinely referred to former Mayor David Dinkins, an African-American, as "the washroom attendant," and who habitually affects an Amos 'n Andy dialect to stereotype blacks as criminals and drug addicts—people he calls "animals" and "mutants."

Here is a flavor of Grant's oratory, as recorded by *Newsday* columnist Paul Vitello.

"The only hope we have is something that we're not brave enough to do. But if there is a brave new world of tomorrow, they will enact the Bob Grant Mandatory Sterilization Plan. [*Adopts mock African-American accent*] I don't have no job, how'm I gonna feed my family?"

Commenting on blacks who attended a celebrity basketball game involving rap stars:

"We have in our nation not hundreds of thousands but millions of sub-humanoids, savages who really would feel more at home careening along the sands of the Kalahari or the dry deserts of eastern Kenya—people who, for whatever reason, have not become civilized."

On the Martin Luther King holiday:

"If they didn't observe Martin King Day, there would be trouble from the savages."

On Haitians living in the United States:

"I wonder if they've ever figured out how they multiply like that. It's like maggots on a hot day. You look one minute and there are so many there, and you look again and wow, they've tripled!"

On refugees fleeing from Haiti:

"The Coast Guard shouldn't pick them up. That's the problem... You know what the ideal situation would be—if they drowned! Then they would stop coming in." (Grant referred to Haitians with AIDS as "vermin" and "subhuman scum.")

Has an aroused press demanded that white politicians denounce Bob Grant's racism and distance themselves from him? Far from it.

New Jersey Gov. Christine Todd Whitman got great publicity for confronting Khalid Muhammad over his anti-Semitism. Has she similarly confronted Grant? No, she appears as a guest on his show, and once thanked Grant for helping her win the election.

What about New York Sen. Alfonse D'Amato—who co-sponsored the Senate resolution denouncing Khalid Muhammad? He's a regular, friendly guest on the Bob Grant program. On one show, the senator encouraged Mayor Dinkins to visit Africa "and stay there."

New York's new mayor, Rudolph Giuliani, has also guested on the show. During one appearance, Grant referred to a black congressman as a "pygmy"; days later, Giuliani said he should have objected to the reference.

Bob Grant is hardly alone in his amplified bigotry against racial minorities or gays or feminists. But such hate is unlikely to get you denounced by the U.S. media and U.S. Senate. More likely, you get your own talk show.

Patrick Buchanan—an admirer of Grant who once called him the "dean of us all"—has long expressed flat-out bigotry against blacks and other groups. That hasn't stopped him from becoming a fixture on TV and radio. Ditto for Rush Limbaugh, who praises Grant in his first book.

And on local talk shows throughout the country, Grant-like shouters spew bigotry against racial minorities.

The evidence suggests that national media are far more bothered by black bigotry than white racism.

Ted Koppel and Bob Grant are co-workers for the same boss, ABC/Capital Cities. Why hasn't Koppel turned a spotlight on Grant? Does he perceive Grant's hate as less pernicious than that of Louis Farrakhan and his lieutenants?

You almost have to pity Khalid Muhammad. If he'd been born white...instead of being denounced by the U.S. Senate, he might have his own major talk show.

March 9, 1994

Spotlight Finally Shines on White Hate Radio

What a difference eight months can make.

Back in March [1994], we wrote a column about powerful radio personality Bob Grant and his brand of hate-filled talkshow. We complained that the rantings of bigots like Grant—who hosts the biggest talkshow on the country's biggest radio station, New York's WABC—were largely ignored or winked at by the mainstream press.

We noted that while national news outlets were fixated on black haters among the Nation of Islam leadership, they were neglecting white racists whose messages are amplified by the largest broadcast stations in the country.

We observed that media commentators kept prodding black politicians to distance themselves from the Louis Farrakhans—but did not ask white politicians to distance themselves from the Bob Grants.

How things have changed...at long last. In recent weeks, news reports spotlighting Grant's on-air racism have appeared prominently in New York media, national outlets, and even the British press.

Over the years, major national advertisers like Sears, Amtrak and Lincoln-Mercury have paid big bucks for access to Grant's 1 million listeners per week. Now, the threat of a sponsor boycott led by African-American ministers has caused several advertisers to pull away from the show.

In past elections, Republican politicians from George Bush on down have cozied up to Grant, seeking his support. Now, his endorsement may be a liability.

The high point of a recent televised debate came when New Jersey Democratic Sen. Frank Lautenberg handed a cassette tape containing samples of Grant's racist remarks to his Republican challenger and demanded that he reject the talkshow host's support. [Lautenberg narrowly won re-election in

1994 after making the Grant issue a major campaign theme.]

A year ago Republican Christine Todd Whitman—who'd just won a close election for New Jersey governor—appeared on Grant's show to thank him for "all that you did to help the campaign." She appeared again two weeks later to personally invite him to her inauguration. Whitman now says she will never again be a guest on Grant's show—unless it's to confront him about his bigotry.

Because Grant has been so successful in building his drive-time audience (he grosses $7 million yearly for his ABC-owned station), he has imitators across the country. As one of the originals in talkshow hate, Grant runs a program that often resembles a Ku Klux Klan rally of the airwaves—cruel, racist, with hints of violence.

Grant espouses a "scientific" form of racism known as eugenics and speaks of the bad "genes" of black youths. He praises City College of New York professor Michael Levin, who asserts that blacks are hereditarily less intelligent than whites.

Never heard the Bob Grant show? Here's the kind of dialogue you're missing.

Caller: "Well, like you say, we'll become a Third World—I think you know, in another 50 or 60 years where everybody is half-black, half-white, and the mentality has gone down around ten IQ points."

Grant: "By the way, we're not supposed to talk about genetics in all of this. And I've been called a lot of names because I do believe in the science of genetics."

When black college students gathered at a New Jersey beach, Grant talked of "the savage mind, the primitive, primordial mentality.... As far as that stretch of beach there at Belmar, it's being written off by, shall we say, civilized people."

The few blacks who call the show can expect to be insulted—and perhaps derided as "shoeshine boys." In hanging up on a black caller, Grant said: "Get off my phone, you creep, we don't need the toilets cleaned right now." When he hangs up on black women, he yells: "I don't need the windows washed today."

When an African-American caller pointed out that the KKK was more violent than the Nation of Islam, Grant hung up on the "swine": "On the evolutionary scale, you're about 25 generations behind me."

Besides verbally abusing callers, Grant continually expresses violent fantasies. "I'd like to get every environmentalist, put 'em up against a wall, and shoot 'em," he once said. In June [1994], he spoke of his wish that police had machine-gunned New York City's gay pride parade. He frequently hopes for the deaths of those he dislikes—Magic Johnson, Bill Clinton, Haitian refugees and others.

His regular listeners cannot escape the violent message. Several months ago, an obviously troubled man phoned the show: "I just wanted to call and vent the hurt and anger I'm experiencing now…. What could I do as a citizen of this country, which I believe in and have seen fall apart as I've been growing up?" Grant's response: "Well, get a gun and go do something, then."

We could say that Bob Grant wannabees have sprouted across the country like mushrooms after a downpour—but that would suggest a wild or natural process. What's happened is something else: a deliberate process in which major broadcasters like ABC/Capital Cities have chosen to narrowcast to conservative audiences by stoking prejudice and fear.

Quaint concepts like decency, fairness and rational debate have been tossed out the window.

The recent uproar over Bob Grant may point to a brighter future. For now, however, on talk radio—the hate just keeps on coming.

[In January 1995, Bob Grant entered national syndication with a weekend show.]

November 2, 1994

Part IV
Violence on Television

"If it bleeds, it leads"—the TV newsroom slogan—is a winning motto for media companies. In the calculus of television programmers and filmmakers, violence is ideal for lucrative broadcasts and commercial hype.

Another Media Celebrity
Charged With Murder

Paul Hill is no O.J. Simpson. His path to media stardom was not athletic greatness and a pleasing public persona. Hill became a media celebrity his own way: by advocating murder.

America was shocked when Simpson became a murder suspect, but it wasn't too surprising when Hill went to jail for killing a doctor and his escort outside a Pensacola, Florida, abortion clinic on July 29 [1994]. After all, the ex-pastor had been advocating such action on major TV shows for over a year.

On television, Hill's belief that a holy book commands the murder of physicians who perform abortions was uttered with the same religious zeal one might expect from those who advocate car-bombings against satanic Westerners.

Except proponents of car-bombing don't get the media forums Hill did.

The point is not that fanatics like Hill should be banned from the airwaves—it's that their extremism ought to be exposed rather than indulged when they do speak on the air.

Appearing as a guest on CNN's *Sonya Live* program on March 8, Hill hailed the man who had murdered abortion provider Dr. David Gunn as a hero "willing to lay down" his life to fulfill "the commandment of Christ."

Host Sonya Friedman responded by seeming to question Hill's commitment to action: "But Mr. Hill, indeed, you personally are not laying down your life. One might suggest that you are offering that message to others and they may be laying down their lives."

Less than five months later, Hill chose action over words, murdering Dr. Gunn's successor at the Pensacola abortion clinic.

Extremism went almost unscathed when Hill appeared on Ted Koppel's *Nightline* on Dec. 8, 1993. Koppel opened the show by comparing legal abortions with violent incidents against abortion clinics—"the latest casualty count" from the abortion "battlefront"—a numerical comparison often made by those who attack clinics: "Thirty million aborted fetuses over the past 30 years [sic] since *Roe v. Wade* was handed down by the Supreme Court. On the other side of the ledger, 7,709 incidents of violence and disruption targeting doctors and abortion clinics since 1977…[including] one attempted murder and one successful murder."

Missing from the numbers were pregnant women—including the estimated 200,000 women who die each year across the globe from *illegal* abortions.

The *Nightline* discussion—which involved only Koppel, Hill and Helen Alvare from the National Conference of Catholic Bishops—was a remarkably polite dialogue on an insane topic: whether killing physicians who perform abortions is justifiable.

While Hill advocated violence to stop abortion, and Alvare didn't, Koppel treated the topic as a legitimate one for serious discussion—allowing Hill to expound at length on his belief that since one can kill to defend a day-old child, it's justifiable to kill an abortion provider.

"God has given us this responsibility," proclaimed Hill, "and if we stand by with our hands in our pockets and watch, say, our wives kill our unborn children, we are actually culpable of not trying to prevent murder… Sometimes you have to use force to stop people from killing innocent children."

Rather than challenge Hill's call for violence, Koppel asserted that Hill had raised an important moral issue: "When we come back, Ms. Alvare, I wonder if you would pick up that very, very difficult moral question, the difference between a child that is one day old and a child that is one day away from birth."

After a commercial break, Koppel acknowledged that abortions are rarely performed in the last months of pregnancy. But he—like his two anti-abortion guests—continued to blur any distinction between a child and a fetus: "If a parent would be justified in using violence, even deadly force, to protect a one-day-old infant," Koppel asked, "why is that same parent not justified in using the same kind of force to prevent the abor-

tion of, let's say, a five-month-old child?"

Had a pro-choice advocate taken part in the discussion, he or she might have mentioned that 99 percent of U.S. abortions occur within the fifth month of pregnancy—and might have challenged Hill's constant equation of terminating a pregnancy with "killing a child." Koppel never did.

When we refer to the morality of doctor-murder as an "insane" topic for TV news forums, we do not mean to imply that Paul Hill is a lone nut.

Hill is hardly alone. Violence against physicians and family planning clinics has been escalating—bolstered by a nationwide movement. Hill's petition defending "lethal force" against doctors had been signed by several dozen priests, ministers and religious activists from around the country.

And while more mainstream "pro-life" leaders were quick to distance themselves from Hill *after* he was charged with murder, he had been invited into their midst for a national strategy meeting in Chicago just three months earlier. The line between advocates and opponents of violence seemed thin; a major discussion item on the meeting's agenda was "Violence and Nonviolence: How to Work With Disagreement."

The gathering was dominated by debates over the morality of killing doctors. "I was surprised at how much support there was for Paul Hill," remarked the director of the Pro-Life Action League. An Operation Rescue leader—who said he argued against murder—told the *New York Times*: "I think I was in the minority."

News media today should be exposing those who turn to violence when they can't win over their fellow citizens through democratic debate. A movement that rationalizes murder as "pro-life" deserves at least as much news coverage as an individual athlete accused of murder.

A floodlight needs to be focused on these extremists. Not merely another spotlight.

August 3, 1994

"Crime Time" News Exploits Fears

"A scary orgy of violent crime is fueling another public call to action."

That's the way *U.S. News & World Report* began its cover story on "Violence in America" in early 1994. In typical fashion, the magazine spoke of "escalating crime numbers" and "the wave of violence" and "the upward spiral" of violent crimes.

It's standard crime coverage: Attention-grabbing, assertive, scary...and inaccurate.

Crime is bad in our country, among the worst in the world—but the Justice Department's crime victimization statistics show there is no more violent crime per capita today than 20 years ago. In 1993, America's crime rate actually fell slightly.

What has soared is crime *coverage*. From 1989 through 1991, the three nightly newscasts on network TV together spent 67 minutes per month on crime. By the end of 1993, "crime time" had more than doubled—to 157 minutes each month.

It's not just the quantity of television coverage, but also the pitch that has been revved up—as the line between tabloid and "quality" TV disappears. The more grisly the footage the better. Aired and re-aired, it can make even the most distant murder seem like right next door.

The media's crime-coverage spree has hit home with the public. According to ABC polling data, only 5 percent named crime as our country's most important problem in June 1993. By February 1994, crime had skyrocketed to problem No. 1—cited by 31 percent of Americans.

Myths and misconceptions abound. *U.S. News & World Report*, for example, warned that violence is a contagion spreading to the suburbs from "coldblooded kids" of "America's mean streets." In fact, crime has been decreasing in the suburbs, according to Justice Department victim statistics.

News reports emphasize the "random" nature of current violence, but less than one-third of murderers are strangers to their victims, according to the FBI; 30 percent of all women murdered in our country are killed by their male partners.

The lurid media coverage pushes politicians to "get tough" on the crime problem. But getting tough is not the same as getting smart. It's often the opposite.

Of course, TV coverage of crime is not about solving problems; it's about grabbing and holding audiences with shock images. If television featured rational discussions, we might have learned by now that the widely touted get-tough "solutions" just aren't working.

Our crime problem would have been solved long ago if more prisons and stiffer sentences were the answers. The United States locks up a larger portion of its people than any other country in the world. Due largely to the "war on drugs," our prison population has almost tripled since 1980—to nearly a million people. Yet there's been no real dent in crime.

With hyped-up coverage treating crime as a sudden crisis, the implication is that there might be a sudden solution—whether it's "three strikes and you're out" from conservatives or gun control from liberals.

But crime is a deep social problem that has developed over decades—and solving it will require confronting issues like youth unemployment, urban decay, racism, child abuse and male violence.

Around the country, crime coverage on local TV news—where the motto is often "if it bleeds, it leads"—can be ghastly. Miami's Fox affiliate, which savors street violence with slow-motion footage and tabloid-style sensationalism, has been censored by some South Florida hotels for scaring the guests.

The Rocky Mountain Media Watch group recently analyzed five days of late-night news on Denver's three network TV affiliates, and found that 54.5 percent of news time was devoted to crime—as were 11 of 15 lead stories and two-thirds of stories over two minutes. While news shows focused on flashing police lights and yellow crime-scene ribbons, issues like homelessness and poverty weren't even covered.

Last month [May 1994], the Los Angeles affiliate of the

media research group FAIR monitored a week of local late-night news on seven TV channels. Crime coverage took up half the news on several outlets. Meanwhile, key regional concerns were virtually ignored—such as a primary election for governor and U.S. senator that was only three weeks away.

Bent on filling air time with crime, Los Angeles stations aired the same story on consecutive nights even when there was no "news," and reached across the country for crime stories—such as a "double execution" in Arkansas and a New Jersey "rampage."

Crime reporting on L.A. stations rarely discussed causes or solutions. Instead, the FAIR survey concluded, it was covered on a "crime-by-crime basis with lots of dramatic visuals." The key seemed to be *entertaining* footage. When surveillance cameras caught a robbery and shooting at a computer store, that footage was shown over and over.

On L.A.'s most crime-saturated outlet, KCBS, the station's own editorialist denounced "body-bag journalism" for contributing to public hysteria about crime. He asserted that violent crime reporting is "easy to do" and "builds readership and ratings."

In some cities, local news programs have pulled back from sensationalizing crime. KIRO-TV in Seattle has pledged to cut all gratuitous crime coverage from its newscasts. A dozen stations, responding to viewer concerns, have followed the lead of WCCO-TV in Minneapolis by inaugurating "family sensitive newscasts" in the 5 p.m. slot. These broadcasts cover crime and violence—minus the gory visuals.

But the real issue goes deeper than how gory the crime coverage should be. It's whether news is about fostering debate on how to solve the problems of our communities—or about creating spectacles that grab our emotions, but keep us on the sidelines...watching.

June 8, 1994

Surprising Reasons for Violence on the Screen

Why is American television so violent?

Forty years after Sen. Estes Kefauver convened the first congressional hearings on the subject, the easy answer is that Americans want to see a lot of violence on the tube. Easy, but erroneous.

The idea that viewers just get what they want "is the biggest fallacy in our business," says maverick TV journalist Linda Ellerbee. "That's the argument that people on our side use to put dreck on the air... The American public didn't ask for trash television. They'll watch it the same way we go out and watch a fire."

In fact, violent TV shows do *not* draw the biggest audiences. The trade magazine *Broadcasting & Cable* noted in 1993 that "the most popular programming is hardly violent, as anyone with a passing knowledge of Nielsen ratings will tell you."

So how come, if you flip the dial tonight, you're likely to see so much gratuitous violence on programs ranging from "real life" cop shows to made-for-TV movies and weekly series? During the past ten years, well over half of prime-time programs have been suffused with violence. Why?

The surprising truth is that violent TV programs are not more popular but they *are* more *profitable*. Much more. Two big reasons: They're cheaper to make, and they're hot export items.

Top creative talent costs money. Well-written scripts, adept acting and sensitive editing are likely to be expensive. It's cheaper to blow up cars in chase scenes and pay for fake blood.

Often, in the United States, the murder-and-mayhem formula does poorly at the box office and in the ratings. However, even if the violent products don't sell very well here, that's just a start.

"The profitable marketing of film and TV programs is increasingly dependent on reaching a global audience," explains longtime researcher George Gerbner, dean emeritus of the Annenberg School for Communications based in Philadelphia.

Investors find that violent screen exports are apt to rake in profits overseas. There's no problem with cross-cultural gaps; whatever the country, viewers get the point. "Everyone understands an action movie," says the producer of the "Die Hard 2" film, in which 264 people get killed. "If I tell a joke, you may not get it, but if a bullet goes through the window, we all know how to hit the floor, no matter the language."

The "Die Hard 2" producer, Larry Gordon, says that syndication firms want "action"—a euphemism for violence—because it "travels well around the world."

Gerbner acknowledges that "there is blood in fairy tales, gore in mythology, murder in Shakespeare. But not all violence is alike." In Televisionland USA, "happy violence" dominates— "produced on the dramatic assembly line...cool, swift, painless and often spectacular, designed not to upset but to deliver the audience to the next commercial in a mood to buy."

Due to public outcries, violence on dramatic network TV programs has dipped a bit during the last three years. Meanwhile, it has escalated on syndicated "real" crime shows.

TV violence remains much more pervasive now than it was back in 1954, when Sen. Kefauver chaired hearings of the Subcommittee on Juvenile Delinquency. And today, politicians and commentators spend a lot more time decrying it.

But the issue is often posed in unhelpful terms: Do violent TV shows and movies lead to high rates of murder, rape and other violent crime? Should Congress legislate restrictions on the violent content of television?

While researchers debate its impacts, few doubt that routine TV violence—particularly the type that presents violent retribution as a pain-free solution to problems—is corrosive to our society.

At the same time, scapegoating television for the crime problem helps elected officials avoid more basic factors—such as the day-in day-out institutionalized violence of poverty and the inadequate funding for education, housing and jobs.

As for government action against the TV industry, the remedy is not content restrictions. Instead, we need antitrust challenges to the fewer and fewer mega-companies that control more and more of the "entertainment" to be found on TV, in video stores and inside theaters.

"The role of Congress, if any," Gerbner says, "is to turn its antitrust and civil rights oversight on to the centralized and globalized industrial structures and marketing strategies that impose violence on creative people and foist it on the children of the world."

The fight that needs to be waged is an *anti*-censorship battle. The violent drivel that fills up screens keeps crowding out better material.

Until we confront the near-monopoly power to saturate the media landscape with mindless violence, the phony blood will keep flowing in torrents, and so will the profits.

September 28, 1994

Part V
Covering (Up) the Environment

In a country where major media owners and advertisers are also major polluters, news about the environment is apt to come too little, too late. Imagine how much better off the Earth would be if those firms devoted as many resources to pollution control as they do to spin control of the news.

Does ABC's *20/20* Close Its Eyes
to Nuclear Stories?

TV news magazine shows like *60 Minutes, PrimeTime Live* and *20/20* pride themselves on their big exposés. But they become quite uncomfortable when their own practices are scrutinized.

A new examination of *20/20*—ABC's top-rated news show hosted by Hugh Downs and Barbara Walters—has found its vision on nuclear and environmental stories to be far less than perfect. Indeed, the show seems to have closed its eyes to certain stories.

In an unusual display of outspokenness about the internal workings of a news program, many current or former *20/20* producers are asserting that the head of the program, executive producer Victor Neufeld, has consistently rejected and discouraged reports on nuclear issues.

And some producers go further: They point to the fact that Neufeld's wife, Lois, is a prominent publicist for the nuclear and chemical industries.

"It was common knowledge among the staff," said Ed Whitmore, a former associate producer at *20/20*, "that Victor's wife was connected to these industries, and the boss wasn't interested in doing environmental stories."

Here are some specific complaints from producers:

- Since Neufeld became *20/20*'s executive producer in 1987, the program has aired only one nuclear-related story—John Stossel's one-sided segment extolling the irradiation of food.

- Neufeld rejected several promising stories on nuclear issues, including one on safety problems at the Rocky Flats nuclear facility in Colorado, and one on new revelations that radioactivity had been discharged at Ohio's Fernald plant—a story *20/20* had covered before Neufeld became boss. "It blew my mind," remarked former *20/20* producer Charles Thompson, "that Victor didn't see the importance of [Fernald]."

- Over the protests of the segment's producer, Neufeld cancelled a dramatic piece on "jumpers"—nuclear maintenance workers who go from plant to plant, absorbing high amounts of radiation.

- During Neufeld's tenure, a number of stories—often reported by John Stossel—have ridiculed environmental concerns. One segment, "Much Ado About Nothing?," minimized the cancer risk of toxic chemicals. Another story, "The Town That Loves Garbage," touted the virtues of landfills.

- A 1991 segment "Allergic to Living" focused on individuals with multiple chemical sensitivities in Texas. Producer Whitmore, who did research on the story, believed the segment to be so heavy-handed in ridiculing the Texans that he warned them before it aired.

The allegations about *20/20*'s allergy to nuclear stories were documented by investigative reporter Karl Grossman for an article in *EXTRA!*, the magazine of the media watch group FAIR. A journalism professor who lectures on media ethics, Grossman is also the author of books critical of the nuclear industry.

Victor Neufeld refused to be interviewed by Grossman or us, but he issued a written statement: "It is inconceivable that I would compromise my own integrity, or that of ABC News, to further the professional or personal gains of anyone close to me, be it my wife, a relative or a friend."

Grossman did interview *20/20* co-host Hugh Downs, who conceded there has been a "paucity of hard-hitting pieces on the environment" on *20/20*, but denied that any "chicanery" was at work.

If Neufeld had taken our calls, we would have asked a simple question: To avoid any appearance of conflict, shouldn't he remove himself from decision-making on 20/20 stories involving the industries his wife champions as a publicist?

Like all good publicists, Lois Neufeld is aggressive. She heads Media Access Inc., and for years has been a leading publicist in New York for the U.S. Council for Energy Awareness, the promotional arm of the nuclear power industry.

A spokesperson for the Council told *EXTRA!* that Lois Neufeld helps TV journalists "get steered where they need to get information, where they need to get industry perspectives, for a story." In April 1989, Victor Neufeld spoke at a conference of the pro-nuclear group.

Later that year, Lois Neufeld was retained by the "Industry Coalition for the Environment," an alliance that includes chemical, petroleum and plastics companies. A key part of her job was to steer TV journalists—including those who worked for her husband—to industry viewpoints in covering the huge 1990 "Earth Day." 20/20 marked Earth Day with a hard-hitting report on pollution…in East Germany.

A publicist who worked with Lois Neufeld for the Industry Coalition praised her inside knowledge of TV news shows, saying she did "a pretty good job of keeping tabs on who was planning to do what, which was important to us."

In 1985, Lois Neufeld picked up early intelligence about an ABC documentary on nuclear power; according to one producer, staffers "resented the interference" when she kept calling about the program, implying "we were getting things wrong."

Asked about conflicts of interest between her work and that of her husband, the publicist responded: "I have my career, and my husband has his, and we are both consummate professionals."

December 15, 1993

Nuclear "Experiments"—Much Wider Than Reported

For several weeks now, news media have provided sensational reports on grisly nuclear experiments by the U.S. government—secret tests such as injections of plutonium, and X-rays of the testicles of prison inmates.

Few stories, however, have shed light on a key truth: Ever since the dawn of the Atomic Age a half-century ago, nuclear activities have involved *large-scale* experimentation on human beings without their voluntary or informed consent.

In August 1945, the U.S. government selected Hiroshima and Nagasaki as ideal sites for measuring the effects of atomic weaponry. Hundreds of thousands of civilians died in those Japanese cities—which were large enough to show the gradations of what a nuclear explosion could do to buildings...and human beings.

The director of the Manhattan Project, Leslie R. Groves, later recalled that it was "desirable that the first target be of such size that the damage would be confined within it, so that we could more definitely determine the power of the bomb."

During the next 17 years, hundreds of U.S. atmospheric bomb tests—in the South Pacific and at the Nevada Test Site— exposed millions of people to intense nuclear fallout...without their informed consent. Cancer, leukemia, and other horrendous effects, including genetic injury, were widespread.

In the Marshall Islands and elsewhere in the Pacific, many native people suffered. So did large numbers of downwind residents in Utah, Nevada and Northern Arizona, plus many of the 300,000 U.S. troops who were exposed to nuclear detonations at close range.

Test site workers suffered similar effects. So did many Native Americans—hired to mine uranium, and sent into what amounted to radon ovens.

Survivors have been left to grieve in silence. As one down-

winder in Southern Utah told us, speaking of government officials: "We bury the dead; they don't."

There have always been a few gutsy journalists struggling
to pull the public-relations mask off of nuclear realities—even
during the height of the Cold War.

Nearly 40 years ago, investigative reporter Paul Jacobs did
research in the vicinity of the Southern Nevada desert, where
mushroom clouds from nuclear blasts rose on a regular basis.

While the big media of the day stuck to the government's
nuclear line, Jacobs—on a shoestring budget—wrote an exceptional in-depth article titled "Clouds from Nevada." Appearing
in *The Reporter* magazine in 1957, his article challenged the safety of open-air nuclear tests. It was prophetic journalism that—if
heeded at the time—would have prevented a great deal of fall-
out-induced harm yet to come.

Two decades later, while at work on a documentary film
updating the story, Jacobs died of cancer. His associates completed the movie, titled "Paul Jacobs and the Nuclear Gang,"
chronicling life and death downwind of the test site.

The documentary won the only Emmy award that PBS
received in 1979. But many TV viewers didn't have a chance to
see "Paul Jacobs and the Nuclear Gang." Under pressure from
nuclear industry groups such as the Atomic Industrial Forum,
nine of the public TV stations in the nation's 24 biggest areas
refused to air the film. (Some other stations postponed it to less
popular time slots.)

Many of the types of experiments making front-page news
these days were documented long ago. In 1986, Rep. Edward J.
Markey released a congressional report titled "American
Nuclear Guinea Pigs: Three Decades of Radioactive Experiments
on U.S. Citizens." But the report got little publicity, in part
because of media deference to the Reagan White House.

As Markey recounted a few weeks ago, "There was a massive public relations partnership that existed between the
administration, the defense contractors and experimenters in
America that worked very effectively throughout the 1980s. I'd say
something and I'd get attacked and it would be a one-day story."

Today, the twin nuclear enterprises of arms production and power plants continue to produce big corporate profits—and massive amounts of radioactive waste.

People living downwind and downriver of nuclear facilities—from Hanford in Washington state to Savannah River in South Carolina—continue to be "guinea pigs."

As the federal government moves to re-tool its nuclear weapons assembly line, plans include the development of "micro-nukes" and "mini-nukes," along with scenarios for "recycling" plutonium and producing tritium for future bombs.

The recent news coverage of horrible experiments, inflicted in past decades on several thousand people, tends to obscure a crucial present-day reality: The entire nuclear cycle—from uranium mining to reactors to atomic waste—remains a mass "nuclear experiment" on us all.

January 12, 1994

M. WUERKER

The Woodstock Story Never Told: Greenpeace vs. Pepsi

SAUGERTIES, N.Y.— One of the great moments of the Woodstock '94 music festival occurred when reggae superstar Jimmy Cliff led thousands in singing his environmental anthem: "Save Our Planet Earth."

With a global audience watching on pay-per-view TV, the angelic Jamaican introduced his song this way: "We got two kinds of people living on this planet—one kind wants to save the planet, while another kind wants to destroy."

Speaking of those who cut down rain forests and pollute the earth, Cliff pointed his finger skyward and declared, "We the people ought to put them under arrest because they are criminals." Many in the young crowd cheered—and joined Cliff in the chorus as he sang of those who pollute: "Stop, you are under arrest... Stop, you are a criminal."

But one Woodstock participant—Pepsico, the festival's main commercial sponsor—was not in tune. TV viewers suddenly found the spirited sing-along interrupted by an ad offering a reminder to "Be Young, Have Fun, Drink Pepsi."

Pepsi's abrupt on-screen appearance was clumsy—yet timely. While no specific polluters are named in Cliff's song, Pepsi was one of the villains singled out by Greenpeace in various festival forums: at its tent in the "Eco-Village"; in a speech from the music stage advising "Make Love, Not Waste"; and on a soaring hot-air balloon that urged Pepsi and other companies to "Clean Up Your Act, Not Your Corporate Image."

Unknown to most festival-goers, Pepsi worked assiduously behind the scenes to muzzle Greenpeace—threatening at one point to withhold financial backing if Greenpeace wasn't reined in. Due to the company's pressure, mini-billboards mentioning Pepsi's role in "The Plastics Recycling Scam" were not displayed.

As a Woodstock '94 sponsor, Pepsi's logo was almost as

ubiquitous as mud at the festival—adorning thousands of plastic soda containers alongside the Woodstock slogan: "2 More Days of Peace and Music." But peace and love gave way to fear and loathing when Pepsi saw its corporate name taken in vain by the likes of Greenpeace.

The educational display in the Greenpeace tent pointed out that Pepsi has been a major plastics polluter since the company moved away from reusable glass bottles years ago. In 1972, there were 288 million plastic (PET) soft drink containers made in the United States. In 1987, there were 6.5 billion produced. The amount of plastics thrown away *each year* in the U.S. has climbed from 400,000 tons in 1960 to 16 million tons in 1990.

With our country overflowing in plastic garbage, Pepsi has begun shifting both production and disposal of plastic bottles to India. Dumping the mess on countries like India is a good way to avoid our environmental and labor laws—but it's exactly the kind of destructive activity that singer Jimmy Cliff wants criminalized.

Rather than bring back glass bottles, Pepsi persists in the production of plastic—which emits toxic chemicals such as chlorinated benzene that can cause cancer and birth defects. Greenpeace claims that producing plastic containers generates at least 100 times more toxic emissions than glass.

Pepsi hails plastic recycling as a solution to the waste problem. But millions of the used plastic bottles exported to Asia are not reprocessed—they are burned or buried. When Greenpeace investigator Ann Leonard visited a plant in India where U.S. soda bottles are shipped, factory officials told her that up to 40 percent could not be recycled.

Disposing of plastic bottles creates big problems whether they are burned (producing dioxin and other toxins) or buried (not biodegradable) or recycled (reprocessing is dirty and dangerous to workers in India and elsewhere.)

The campaign urging Pepsi to return to reusable glass bottles is part of Greenpeace's Toxic Trade Project—targeting corporations that dump waste in Africa, Asia and Latin America rather than convert to clean production at home. Nearly 2,000

Woodstock concertgoers signed postcards to Pepsi's CEO: "The so-called 'Pepsi Generation' wants the planet to survive for countless more generations."

Speaking from the music stage, Harvey Wasserman of Greenpeace told the crowd: "Yours is a generation of choice. Your choice is not between Pepsi and Coke, RC and iced tea. Your choice is between a world drowning in plastic versus one based on renewables and recycling."

With its message that "This Planet Is Not For Sale," Greenpeace hoped to instill in Woodstock '94 the spirit of the 1969 concert. But 25 years ago, Woodstock had no corporate sponsors.

Nowadays, through advertising and sponsorship strategies, companies with dubious environmental policies are able to "greenwash" their images to appear ecologically responsible. One method is by hailing faulty "recycling" efforts.

Pepsico—which underwrites the *MacNeil/Lehrer NewsHour* and other TV news and public affairs shows—apparently saw its festival sponsorship as buying censorship of criticism. But Woodstock promoter Michael Lang saw it differently, and let a Greenpeace leader speak from the stage.

Corporate sponsorship holds more sway over news media than over music concerts. Perhaps that's why the American public is so well-informed about allegations against celebrities like Michael Jackson and Tonya Harding, but so uninformed about accusations against corporate celebrities like Pepsi.

We hope to see the Greenpeace-Pepsi dispute included in the Woodstock '94 movie—which, thankfully, is not sponsored by Pepsi. Maybe we'll even get to see Jimmy Cliff singing "Save Our Planet Earth"...without commercial interruption.

August 17, 1994

Part VI
Public Health

Enormous amounts of media space are devoted to health-related topics, from government policies to personal choices. The spin behind the news, however, often has a way of being hazardous to our health—and protective of big profit margins.

It's Time for a Real Debate
on National Health Insurance

When a coalition of groups concerned about health care held a loud public protest in midtown Manhattan on May 12 [1993], they didn't set up their picket line outside a hospital or insurance company headquarters or government agency.

Instead, they gathered in front of the *New York Times* building, and their demand was simple: "Stop rationing health care news!" The protesters are angry over the fact that the newspaper's reporting routinely downplays a popular proposal—endorsed by 12 of New York City's 14 members of Congress—to overhaul the American health system: *a single-payer system of publicly-financed health care.*

Poll after poll has shown that most Americans favor tax-financed national health insurance. But at the *New York Times* and other national media, proponents are kept at the periphery of the health care debate. They include 58 members of Congress who, on March 3 [1993], introduced a bill—"The American Health Security Act"—to establish a Canadian-style, single-payer system.

In a single-payer system, private insurance companies are basically removed from health care. Instead, the government pays all health care providers, and controls fees and costs. As in Canada, consumers would choose their own doctors—but almost never receive a hospital or doctor bill. Insurance deductibles and co-payments are also eliminated.

By eliminating administrative waste and insurance company profits, the shift to a single-payer system would cut $67 billion per year from our country's medical bill, according to the General Accounting Office—and $39 billion yearly in bureaucracy, according to the Congressional Budget Office. Of every health-care dollar spent in the U.S., 22 cents goes to administrators; in Canada, that figure is 10 cents.

A single-payer system has been endorsed by health care

activists, seniors groups, labor unions and a number of regional dailies—including the *Atlanta Journal-Constitution* and St. Louis *Post-Dispatch*. A recent Times-Mirror poll found 41 percent of U.S. doctors in support.

After conducting extensive focus groups on health care, pollster Celinda Lake discovered that the more people are told about the Canadian system, "the higher the support goes." In contrast, according to Lake, working Americans found the *managed competition* idea "laughable."

But much of the national news coverage in recent weeks has been promoting Bill Clinton's managed competition plan as the smart, new, "politically viable" option.

News reports trumpet the "consensus" behind managed competition: big insurance companies, most doctors, conservative Republican think tanks, George Bush, conservative Democratic think tanks, Hillary Rodham Clinton—and the wise men from the "Jackson Hole Group" who've been meeting in Wyoming for years to discuss "health care reform."

In national media discourse, managed competition seems easier to tout than explain. Since no other country has ever tried such a system, it remains a complicated, untested theory.

The plan leaves the largest insurance companies in the center of the picture; after the federal government defines a minimum package of benefits, health care partnerships or super-HMOs organized by insurance firms would "compete" to offer health packages. Meanwhile, giant "Health Insurance Purchasing Cooperatives" would be formed so that employers and consumers could search for the best deal. Between these behemoths would be the government, "managing the competition," grading the medical providers and trying to restrain costs.

To the protesters outside the *New York Times* headquarters, the news tilt toward managed competition is explained by the clout of insurance companies and medical industry firms—which are major media advertisers. And, as it happens, four members of the *New York Times* board of directors are also directors of major insurance companies; two are directors of pharmaceutical companies.

The New York Times

Hillary Clinton's Potent Brain Trust On Health Reform

Some of the Jackson Hole Group members who gathered last weekend: At left, the founder, Paul Ellwood, in whose home the group meets; from left on couch, William Link (Prudential), Lawrence English (Cigna), Dan Roble (an attorney), Charles Buck (General Electric), David Scherb (Pepsico); behind, from left, James Todd (American Medical Association), Paul Freiman (Pharmaceutical Manufacturers Association), David Lawrence (Kaiser), Robert Hansberger (Voluntary Hospitals of America) and James McLane (Aetna).

New York Times, Feb. 28, 1993, on how the Jackson Hole group's managed competition scheme was *helping* Hillary Clinton to reform health care.

While it's far-fetched to hunt for a conspiracy, the imprint of the insurance industry is all over the managed competition idea. The Jackson Hole study group that originated the scheme is made up of big insurance companies like Prudential, Metropolitan Life, Aetna and Cigna, plus hospital and pharmaceutical interests. Insurers were important early contributors to Clinton's presidential campaign, and donated $850,000 to the Democratic Party (and even more to the Republicans) for the 1992 elections.

Critics dismiss managed competition as a bureaucratic hoax that should be renamed the "Insurance Industry Preservation Act." They warn that the freedom to choose one's own doctor would be eroded. They say it's absurd to leave "reform" to the Jackson Hole group of special interests who profit from the inefficient status quo.

Managed competition was the subject of a lengthy *MacNeil/Lehrer NewsHour* discussion on May 5 [1993]. The panel was made up of three government officials—a congressman, a governor and a state health commissioner—who said the Clinton approach would lower costs, and a fourth panelist, Dr. Steffie Woolhandler, who argued it would increase costs and bureaucracy. (Woolhandler founded Physicians for a National Health Program, representing thousands of doctors who support a single-payer system.)

Near the end of the discussion, anchor Robert MacNeil offered Woolhandler the last word "since you're in the minority"—to which she responded: "Robert, I'm not in a minority. Polls are showing two-thirds of the American people support government-funded national health insurance."

MacNeil then rephrased his question: "If this [managed competition] is the program that has a political consensus and the other one that you advocate [single-payer] is considered impossible politically at the moment, why are you then against the one that is viable?"

Because it won't "provide Americans with the care they need," the doctor replied.

But she could have offered another response: *If much of the public supports national health insurance, and it's not debated seriously in Washington or the national media because of the power of special interests like the insurance lobby, what does that say about the health of our democracy?*

That is an issue journalists should be exploring.

May 12, 1993

Media Myth Pits Clinton
Against Insurance Industry

Buoyed by NAFTA's victory, the White House will now concentrate on its other major policy initiative—health care reform. We can expect mainstream news outlets to paint a picture of Bill and Hillary Clinton in mortal battle against the big bad insurance industry.

It's a vivid picture, but it distorts reality. As in the NAFTA battle, big corporations are in the president's corner.

In a much-publicized campaign aimed at whipping up populist support for the administration's health plan, Hillary Rodham Clinton blasted insurance companies opposing it. She denounced their "homey kitchen ads" airing on TV—featuring complaints from "Harry" and "Louise" about the Clinton plan. "There must be a better way," laments Louise.

"What you don't get told in the ad," charged Hillary Clinton, "is that it is paid for by insurance companies... It is time for you and every American to stand up and say to the insurance industry: 'Enough is enough, we want our health care system back!'"

The Democratic Party countered with its own ad promoting the White House plan: "The insurance companies may not like it, but the president didn't design it for them."

The rhetoric was hot—and the TV networks swallowed it hook, line and salsa. NBC's Tom Brokaw spoke of Hillary Clinton's "scathing attack on the health insurance industry." A CNN anchor declared that the administration was "engaged in something close to all-out war with the health insurance industry."

A full-blown media myth was born, with most reports omitting basic facts:

- The Health Insurance Association of America, which opposes the Clinton plan and produced the Harry and

Louise ads, represents *small to medium-size* insurance companies. They would lose out to bigger firms under the administration's "managed competition" plan.

- The "Big Five" of health insurers—Aetna, Cigna, Metropolitan Life, Prudential and Travelers—have formed the Alliance for Managed Competition, which is sympathetic to the Clinton plan. That's because those firms, heavily invested in Health Maintenance Organizations, would be enriched by it.

- Operating through the Jackson Hole study group, the insurance giants helped draw up the managed competition blueprint, later adopted by the Clinton administration. Contrary to the Democratic Party ads, the Clinton plan was designed for—and by—big insurance interests. In a 1992 article in *Health Economics* magazine, Jackson Hole leaders bluntly argued that managed competition is the only way to avert a government takeover of "health care financing" and the "elimination of a multiple-payer private insurance industry."

What the Jackson Hole group feared was a Canadian-style system in which the government (the "single-payer") controls costs while paying all hospital and doctor bills. Single-payer rids health care of private insurance companies—along with costly bureaucracy, profiteering and wasteful advertising.

Despite the fact that a single-payer proposal has been endorsed by 95 members of Congress—plus groups like Consumers Union and Public Citizen—most major media have pushed it to the margins. A recent computer search found only one mention of the single-payer proposal on ABC's *World News Tonight* in all of 1993.

When media do mention a Canadian-style system, it's often dismissed as "politically unrealistic." Yet according to General Accounting Office and Congressional Budget Office studies, only single-payer has a *realistic* chance of extending universal coverage without raising costs—the goal politicians claim to be seeking.

In a *MacNeil/Lehrer NewsHour* segment about the various ads debating health care reform, anchor Margaret Warner proclaimed that "interest groups on all sides of the issue have taken to the airwaves."

Not quite.

One ad, supporting a single-payer system, has been kept off the airwaves from San Francisco to Boston to Washington, D.C. Produced by the grassroots group Neighbor to Neighbor, the ad features an engaging elderly woman, who asserts: "If we get rid of health insurance companies, we can have complete coverage for everyone for the same money. But any plan that keeps these guys in business will cost billions... To me, it's a no-brainer."

TV station managers offered a variety of excuses for rejecting the ad ("it's a call to action"; "too broad"; "undocumented"). According to Neighbor to Neighbor, one station executive candidly explained: "Many of our major advertisers are health insurers. We don't want to take any hits from the insurance companies."

While one side can't even buy its way into the debate, many news outlets offer a narrow health-care discussion pitting the Clinton plan—supported by large insurers—against smaller insurance companies that oppose it.

Something's wrong with a spectrum of debate no broader than the confines of the insurance industry.

November 24, 1993

Women and AIDS:
A Magazine's Bad Advice

If you've ever wondered whether irresponsible media can be deadly, consider the sad story of *Cosmopolitan* magazine and women with AIDS.

A federal report disclosed on July 22 [1993] that heterosexual contact, not drug needles, is now the leading cause of AIDS among women in the United States. And figures show more women than ever—6,642 last year—diagnosed with new cases of AIDS.

For women—who are much more vulnerable than men to infection with the AIDS virus during heterosexual intercourse—occurrences of sexual transmission have more than doubled since 1988. According to the Centers for Disease Control, most of the infected women have been "sex partners of injecting-drug users," with rates highest among black women.

Back in 1988, *Cosmopolitan* published an article titled "Reassuring News About AIDS: A Doctor Tells Why You May Not Be At Risk." The magazine declared that "there is almost no danger of contracting AIDS through ordinary sexual intercourse."

Written by Dr. Robert E. Gould, the article disputed what it called "the false impression that an IV drug user passes the AIDS virus on to his or her partner through vaginal intercourse."

Enthusiastic about fashion and romance, *Cosmopolitan*—like many magazines—strives to provide articles in sync with the upbeat mood of advertisements. In *Cosmo*'s case, that means lots of emphasis on sex.

Gould's article decried "the continually mounting fear and false alarm that may make it difficult for any of us to enjoy sex." Soon afterward, the magazine's editor Helen Gurley Brown defended the article on national TV.

"We have come so far in relieving women of fear and fright

and guilt," she said, "and now along comes this thing to scare the daylights out of everybody forever. And since there isn't too much proof that AIDS is spread through heterosexual intercourse, I think our side should be presented, too."

Brown was speaking on the ABC program *Nightline*. Host Ted Koppel zeroed in on the key point during the Jan. 21, 1988 broadcast: "When your readership, ten million mostly young women, read an article like that, and draw the conclusion that therefore, maybe they don't need to urge their partners to use condoms, do you feel entirely comfortable with that?"

"I feel quite comfortable with this," Brown replied.

Are we unfairly condemning the *Cosmopolitan* article now, based on information that Helen Gurley Brown didn't have access to at the time? Not at all.

As soon as the January 1988 article came off the press, medical authorities on AIDS denounced it. "I would characterize it clearly as not based on the known facts," said Dr. Anthony Fauci of the National Institutes of Health. He termed the article "really potentially dangerous" for claiming that "if you don't have vaginal or penile lesions, you won't catch the AIDS virus by vaginal intercourse."

C. Everett Koop, then Surgeon General, singled out the *Cosmopolitan* article when he told a hearing on Capitol Hill a few weeks later: "It is just not true that there is no danger from normal vaginal intercourse." Mathilde Krim of the American Foundation for AIDS Research also disputed the article's contentions at the time.

Despite all the criticism, since then *Cosmopolitan* has devoted scant coverage to AIDS risks. And the magazine continued its don't-worry be-happy approach by publishing a lengthy article in March 1992, "AIDS: The Real Story About Risk," which again downplayed AIDS dangers.

Sometimes, for ideological reasons, political commentators have also denied the reality that AIDS puts most people at risk. In November 1991, Patrick Buchanan wrote a scornful syndicated column about what he called "the myth of heterosexual AIDS."

Promoting his political theology of hatred toward gay people, Buchanan complained about those who "want to ignore the traditional morality, but never pay the price." A few months later, campaigning for the Republican presidential nomination, Buchanan told radio listeners: "AIDS is nature's retribution for violating the laws of nature."

With AIDS afflicting friends, lovers, brothers, sisters, sons, daughters, fathers and mothers, it's crucial that we challenge both wishful thinking and bigotry. Then maybe we can concentrate on supporting people with AIDS while fighting the disease.

The author of the CDC's latest report, Dr. Pascale Wortley, told us that past indications of widening AIDS risks were often "the kind of thing that people just didn't want to believe." But instead of telling us what we'd prefer to believe, media have a responsibility to tell us what we need to know.

July 28, 1993

Tributes to Randy Shilts
Ignored His Media Criticism

After Randy Shilts died in mid-February [1994], news stories remembered him as a pathbreaking journalist who overcame two huge obstacles—prejudice against gay people and ignorance of AIDS.

Media retrospectives hailed Shilts as an openly gay reporter who broke new ground after joining the staff of a large daily newspaper in 1981. Shilts played a historic role for gays in big-league journalism, comparable to Jackie Robinson's role for blacks in major-league baseball.

Reporting for the *San Francisco Chronicle*, Shilts exposed the AIDS epidemic early on. That put him in conflict with many heterosexuals inclined to ignore the deadly disease because it mainly struck homosexuals. And Shilts also angered some gay men who resented his candid articles about sexual transmission of AIDS.

A few days after Shilts died from AIDS at age 42, the CBS TV program *60 Minutes* featured a moving interview with him. But such media reports on the life and death of Randy Shilts routinely omitted his sharp criticisms of mainstream journalism—for shoddy coverage of AIDS, and for tacit acceptance of anti-gay attitudes.

His landmark book *And the Band Played On*—documenting indifference and duplicity during the first years of the AIDS epidemic—gained accolades when it was published in 1987. Yet, by the decade's end the nationwide volume of AIDS news coverage had dropped to its lowest level in three years. "One consequence," Shilts wrote in 1989, "is that CDC [Centers for Disease Control] staffers now routinely find that many people think the AIDS epidemic has 'leveled out' or peaked."

The reality, he added, was quite different: "Caseloads have never been higher, with as many as 1,400 Americans a week being diagnosed with the disease. It is only the media's interest that has peaked."

When the 1980s drew to a close, Shilts noted that "no TV network has a reporter covering AIDS full-time." And he used the word *dismal* to describe "the state of print reporting on federal AIDS policy."

Shilts was no firebrand; in fact, many gay-rights activists considered him conservative.

But Shilts could be blunt, as when he declared: "Inarguably, the fact that gay men were the epidemic's first identified casualties had everything to do with how this country initially responded to the disease. Most of the institutional failures to confront the epidemic aggressively—whether in science, government or the media—can be traced to prejudice against gays."

That prejudice surged into the national spotlight in early 1993. Although large numbers of gays have always been in the U.S. armed forces, the possibility that they would no longer be forced to stay in the closet sent homophobes into a protracted frenzy.

(Shilts' exhaustive 1993 book, *Conduct Unbecoming*, exposed the sordid history of U.S. military witchhunts against service men and women suspected of being gay.)

In the summer of 1993, as Senate hearings paved the way for continued discrimination against gays in the military, listeners to KPFA Radio in the San Francisco area heard an interview with Randy Shilts—expressing views on the press that never made it into his obituaries.

The tone of those hearings, said Shilts, "showed how profoundly ignorant our society remains. And it shows that among our sort of intelligentsia, the pundit class and things, for there not to be absolute outrage at what's being said in these hearings is—I find it astounding."

Shilts added: "The *New York Times* even wrote a story saying, 'Gee this is an issue that's emotional but these hearings have been calm and rational.'" He laughed dryly. "Well, everybody's up there talking about how gay men are going to be raping everybody in the showers. I mean, in polite codewords, but that's basically what they're saying. And I just can't believe that there's no outrage among sort of the liberal media class…. They'll write editorials saying gays should be allowed in, but there's no sense of outrage about what this ban means."

The ban "basically says that if you're gay, you're presented with a list of jobs in our society that you are not permitted to hold, no matter how well you're qualified and no matter what the content of your character is…. This is not something that's supposed to happen in a free society. And that's what this ban means to me. It just shows that we're not a free society."

Even today, the trails that Shilts blazed are still choked with prejudice.

Just ask Sandy Nelson, an award-winning journalist in the fourth year of battling to get her reporting job back at the *Morning News Tribune*—owned by the McClatchy newspaper chain—in Tacoma, Washington. Nelson, a lesbian, was transferred involuntarily to a copy-editor post because of off-duty activities for gay rights.

Just ask the activists fighting for more funds for AIDS prevention, while the Clinton administration proposes to cut those funds and the news media pay little attention.

And ask gay people—in the military and in a wide range of other workplaces—who live under intense pressure to hide their sexual orientation.

Meanwhile, anti-gay ballot initiatives proliferate in many states.

Randy Shilts achieved a great deal before his death. But the bigotry that he challenged is still very much alive.

February 23, 1994

Is Tobacco Money Muffling the Press?

When *Newsweek* ran a cover story last month about "The Hunt for the Breast Cancer Gene," no one could doubt the humanitarian message. But the magazine's full-color back cover was devoted to a less noble purpose—selling cigarettes.

The causes of breast cancer may be somewhat unclear—but the same can't be said about lung cancer, which now kills more American women than any other form of cancer. Cigarettes are causing many of those deaths. And women are key targets of the multibillion-dollar cigarette ad industry.

"The cigarette is often offered as an emblem of independence and nonconformity," says advertising researcher Jean Kilbourne. "Teenage girls are especially vulnerable to this pitch."

Ads aimed at female adolescents seem to be working. "Twenty percent of young women graduating from high school smoke, versus 10 percent of men," Kilbourne points out. And overall, about 90 percent of the new smokers in this country are teenage or younger.

To make matters worse, young readers who leaf through women's magazines are apt to find plenty of ads glorifying cigarettes, but hardly any articles about the dreadful health effects of tobacco.

A few weeks ago, community medicine specialist John P. Pierce of the University of California at San Diego released data showing an increase in smoking among teenagers because of the cartoonish Joe Camel ads put out by R.J. Reynolds. "The issue here," he said, "is to protect our children from being influenced into an addiction that will cause cancer."

With the cigarette industry posing such a serious public health threat, a few media pundits go out of their way to denounce it. And a laudable minority of newspapers and magazines refuse to run cigarette ads. But for the most part, it's tobacco business as usual, with more than $4 billion spent on cigarette advertising each year.

Sometimes it's not even possible to *buy* space for a strong anti-smoking message, as a group called Stop Teenage Addiction to Tobacco found out recently.

The organization put together a provocative ad: "Meet Five of America's Richest Drug Pushers," said the headline— over pictures of media tycoons S.I. Newhouse, Rupert Murdoch and CBS chairman Laurence Tisch (who owns a big chunk of Lorillard Tobacco), along with Henry Kravis of R.J. Reynolds and Michael Miles, chair of Philip Morris.

The text of the advertisement posed a question and answered it: "What do all five of these men have in common? Like most 'drug pushers,' they're smart enough not to use the product they sell. Not one of them smokes cigarettes."

The ad went on: "Si, Rupert, Larry, Henry, Mike: If you'll agree it's crazy for a society to *promote* its leading cause of pre-ventable death, and stop doing it, we'll take out an ad twice as big honoring you and saying thanks. There's no greater contri-bution you could make to America's health."

The *New York Times* turned down the ad, insisting that it could not run unless the headline were eliminated along with the five photos and names. It seems that the *Times* has a prohi-bition against strong anti-smoking ads—though it runs strong pro-smoking ads on a regular basis.

According to researcher Steven Bishofsky, who recently interviewed the advertising managers of more than 50 maga-zines, fear of losing revenue from tobacco interests leads many publications to shy away from anti-smoking ads.

Bishofsky, a graduate student at the University of Washington's School of Communications, learned that even magazines refusing cigarette ads seemed intimidated—worried about offending "the tobacco parent company." Almost 60 per-cent of the magazine executives told Bishofsky about their advertising accounts from subsidiaries of tobacco companies, such as Kraft/General Foods (Philip Morris) and Nabisco Foods (R.J. Reynolds).

"The cigarette is an incredible cash cow," commented Michael Pertschuk, former chair of the Federal Trade

Commission. "The cigarette companies make enormous amounts of money, and that is the major reason they are buying up the rest of the consumer goods businesses in the United States. Philip Morris has enough money that with its spare change it picks up General Foods and Kraft, and that creates and extends its network of influence, power and money."

Pertschuk—who contends that all cigarette advertising fits FTC definitions of "deceptive" and "unfair"—says that "anyone who thinks cigarette advertising is about information still believes in the tooth fairy. Cigarette advertising is about imagery, seductive imagery."

The seduction is part of a deadly industry's insatiable quest for profits. And many media outlets function as accomplices.

January 5, 1994

Part VII
Prejudice and the Media Curve

The media power to define social problems—and call for solutions—rests overwhelmingly in the hands of people who are insulated from the negative effects of chronic inequities and ongoing discrimination.

Newsweekly Job Slot:
White Guys Who Lecture Blacks

Two of this country's big weekly newsmagazines have regular columnist slots for white men fixated on lecturing about the moral failures of black people, especially in the inner city.

The second week of August [1994] was typical. While *Newsweek* columnist Joe Klein provided yet another treatise on ghetto depravity, *U.S. News & World Report* columnist John Leo was again decrying the debasement of standards by people with dark skin and meager merit.

George Will might have joined in on the last page of *Newsweek*, but his biweekly column was off for the Aug. 15 issue.

"The problem isn't the absence of jobs, but the culture of poverty," proclaimed the *Newsweek* headline over Joe Klein's run-through of trusty buzz phrases—"welfare dependency...out-of-wedlock births to teenagers...irresponsible, antisocial behavior that has its roots in the perverse incentives of the welfare system..."

We await the *Newsweek* headline, "The problem isn't the absence of food, but the culture of hunger."

After his familiar windup, Klein came in with his closing pitch—concluding that "the absence of responsible parents, especially fathers, is the phenomenon at the heart of underclass poverty." Such media critiques of deadbeat dads have a way of letting a deadbeat government off the hook.

Meanwhile, inside *U.S. News & World Report,* John Leo was carrying one of his favorite tunes with as much ease as Bing Crosby crooning "White Christmas." It was another ode to the way things used to be—in this case, the good old days at the City University of New York—contrasted with the degraded present-day results of "ever lowering standards" and "large dollops of multiculturalism."

The villain of Leo's piece was that old reliable bête noire:

"affirmative action."

It's a hobbyhorse that George Will has been riding across the pages of *Newsweek* for nearly two decades. In 1985, he lashed out at remedies for unequal opportunity as a "racial spoils system that has grown behind the perfumed phrase 'affirmative action.'" Will complained: "The acid of 'race conscious' policies has been seeping into the law, eroding a bedrock principle of this republic, the principle that rights inhere in individuals, not groups." He ignored other *bedrock principles of this republic:* slavery, and then legally-sanctioned racial discrimination which continued into the 1960s.

George Will evidently liked the phrase "racial spoils system" so much that he re-deployed it in February 1991, blasting "the quagmire of counting by race in order to engineer 'correct' balances here, there and everywhere.... The rickety structure of affirmative action, quotas and the rest of the racial spoils system depends on victimology—winning for certain groups the lucrative status of victim."

This is a popular theme: minorities as rip-off artists, playing on the guilt and gullibility of whites who—if Klein, Leo and Will are to be believed—are the real victims these days.

Leo and Will, in particular, also express notable hostility toward feminists. Leo recently told a San Francisco radio audience that most women's studies departments on U.S. campuses are staffed by "man-haters."

Meanwhile, these pontificators see female heads of households as fair game. Millions of women with little income and much determination are made the objects of resentment, innuendo and thinly veiled derision.

When Joe Klein wrote last year that "out-of-wedlock births to teenagers are at the heart of the nexus of pathologies that define the underclass," he did not find the space to mention white racism as any kind of pathology at all.

Klein, Leo and Will spearhead a pundit brotherhood that largely consigns white racism to the past (it's a "legacy" in Klein's Aug. 15 *Newsweek* column), giving it little mention while getting to the point—which is often that white people are being mistreated and hustled by less principled elements of society.

So, in the July 4 issue of *U.S. News & World Report*, a John Leo sentence that takes off with "Bias is real, but…" ends with an all-too-familiar touchdown about "our elaborate victim culture."

A shared theme is that wily civil rights activists are concocting racial and gender bias to fatten their coffers. George Will in *Newsweek*, Feb. 11, 1991: "Some black leaders and their white allies have a political interest in regarding blacks, and getting blacks to regard themselves, as victims who must be wards of government…"

From their newsweekly pulpits, the white men in silk ties thunder on about immorality in low places. "Suddenly the nation sees that its most important problem is the conjunction of illegitimacy and welfare dependency," George Will declared in *Newsweek* this spring.

"The incessant emphasis on the dysfunctioning of black people," National Council of Negro Women president Dorothy I. Height has noted, "is simply one more attempt to show that African-Americans do not really fit into the society—that we are 'overdependent' and predominantly welfare-oriented. Quite overlooked in this equation is the fact that most black Americans are, on the contrary, overwhelmingly among the working poor."

Says scientist Stephen Jay Gould: "How convenient to blame the poor and the hungry for their own condition—lest we be forced to blame our economic system or our government for an abject failure to secure a decent life for all people."

We await the day when even one black commentator at *Newsweek*, or *U.S. News & World Report*, or *Time*, has a regular column to shed light on the continuing toll taken by racism and economic injustice in the present day.

August 10, 1994

Dodging the Deeper News
of Inner-City Violence

Speculation that Los Angeles might again go up in flames dominated coverage of the recent federal trial of police officers who beat Rodney King. When the verdict came in and no riot ensued, national media gave a cheer and moved on.

The possibility of inner-city burning and looting and mayhem is big news: worthy of live, round-the-clock broadcasts and spare-no-expense news coverage.

But no TV vans with satellite uplinks surround an underfunded county hospital where poor children wait hour after hour for inadequate medical care. Nor do viewers see many breathless live news reports from the lines at unemployment offices or the welfare department.

Reporting that mentions malnutrition or untreated disease or chronic joblessness is often low-key and matter-of-fact. Such problems are not really "news" so much as permanent scenery on the social landscape.

Front pages rarely focus on routine institutional violence—such as dilapidated ghetto housing that is profitable for owners who don't live there and dehumanizing for people who do.

In most media coverage of urban ills, the spotlight is on poor people as *the problem*—not on business or governmental decisions that enforce extreme inequities.

The plight of poor people is sometimes chronicled with compassion and painful detail. But key questions go unasked.

Such as: What individuals or corporate entities—banks, manufacturers, absentee landlords, realtors, etc.—profit from the stark conditions that mean such awful poverty and circumscribed opportunity for some people because of their race and dire economic straits?

Though rarely mentioned in big media, there are links between bloated wealth and anemic poverty. What fattens some investors is apt to come at the expense of the impoverished.

An emerging "public-private partnership" to solve urban woes has gained plenty of media hype lately. For the most part it is a fairy tale.

A year after Los Angeles exploded in April 1992, unemployment is still rife, and no real improvement is on the horizon. Promises that "the private sector" would provide new opportunities have turned to ashes. Although press releases proliferated from companies pledging investment and job creation, actual dollars have been meager.

Last summer General Motors announced $15 million in contracts for inner-city suppliers of an aircraft subsidiary, a move that might end up creating a few hundred jobs in Los Angeles. A month later, to considerably less fanfare, GM closed its last auto assembly plant in L.A.; some 3,000 workers, most of them black or Latino, lost their jobs with the flick of a corporate pen.

Ironically, perhaps the most powerful "public-private partnership" is between government officials and corporate media avoiding central truths about power in our society.

James Baldwin wrote a quarter-century ago that "any real commitment to black freedom in this country would have the effect of reordering all our priorities." He added that "what we call a race problem here is not a race problem at all." The central problem involves brutal social policies that perpetuate massive deprivation in housing, education, nutrition, health care and economic opportunity.

National priorities remain cemented to the old order. Some conditions have worsened. In 1970, the unemployment rate for black workers was 86 percent greater than that of white workers. In 1990, it was 176 percent greater.

During his last years, Martin Luther King Jr. alienated former allies in the mainstream press by connecting poverty and racism to militarism. He saw that priorities—how society appropriated its resources—prefigured results.

Vague rhetoric aside, Bill Clinton does not see ending poverty as a priority. And that's how mass media pundits like it.

Clinton's budget would cut only a few billion dollars in

military spending next year. Yet the Center for Defense Information, headed by retired U.S. military officers, says that $30 billion could be quickly freed up for domestic social programs simply "by canceling unneeded Cold War weapons and accelerating the withdrawal of U.S. troops from foreign countries."

In fact, CDI says, more than $50 billion could be cut from the Clinton military budget during *each* of the next five years. But you won't hear much of this analysis; it's off the media map. Instead, we hear raging debates about whether Clinton's paltry jobs program is too expensive.

A war on poverty is one battle America's governing elites would rather not fight. And so the daily status quo—which amounts to a war against the poor—grinds on.

Unfortunately for the future, there's little indication that national news media will cover the issue of poverty with the same intensity as their recent overblown violence-watch in Los Angeles.

April 21, 1993

Big News Media Flee the Cities

"Most metropolitan newspapers," Chicago mayor Harold Washington said shortly before his death, "do not cater to the working public within their cities; they reach out to the suburbs to embrace a more affluent readership."

Mayor Washington was speaking eight years ago. Since then, on the whole, the situation he described has gotten worse: "These papers are still based in our cities, they own city property and to a great extent they control our cities. But newspapers largely ignore the people right around them."

Preoccupied with demographic data, many media owners are fixated on audiences with higher incomes. Top editors and broadcast producers often find themselves under pressure to attract the kind of upscale readers, viewers and listeners valued by advertisers.

This quest tends to leave many city dwellers in the lurch. Usually the transition is gradual, but occasionally it's dramatic—as when, almost overnight, the orientation of the *Oakland Tribune* went from urban to suburban.

During the 1980s, the *Tribune* was a rarity; its publisher Robert Maynard, a seasoned journalist, was a visible part of Oakland's black community. But in 1992, facing a financial crisis and a personal battle with cancer, Maynard sold the paper to a suburban chain. Since then, less ink has gone to the low-income people who comprise so much of Oakland.

The trend at many news outlets is to gloss over the day-to-day experiences of living in a city, as distinct from merely working or unwinding there. An outspoken editor at *USA Today*, Barbara Reynolds, describes the news media's "rule of thumb for covering cities" this way: "Ho-hum, they're still poor—old story, no news."

The ho-hum attitudes coincide with a lack of diversity among media management. Some progress has been made, but the latest [1994] figures from the American Society of Newspaper Editors show that racial minorities account for only

7.7 percent of newsroom supervisors. (People of color comprise about 25 percent of the public.)

In national news media, the poor and moderate-income people who inhabit America's urban centers are increasingly under-reported—unless, of course, they can serve as characters in another dramatic story on violent crime or welfare abuse.

Researcher Andrew Tyndall, publisher of the *Tyndall Report* newsletter, added up all the time that network TV nightly newscasts spent on stock market fluctuations. Then he totaled the air time that the same news programs spent on problems of poverty.

The results? "Over the last four years, the network news time-count shows 675 minutes about the poor versus 707 tracking the assets of the rich."

One reason for the scant coverage of inner-city residents is that they're virtually ignored in national politics. Mass media depict the chronically unemployed and under-employed as irrelevant in the corridors of power. "The country is not clamoring for a jobs bill," proclaimed the liberal pundit Christopher Matthews on CBS's *Face the Nation* in 1993.

The election of Bill Clinton—who had pledged federal jobs programs and urban aid—lifted hopes in city halls and neighborhoods desperate for help. But pundits voiced fears that the new president might actually fulfill his campaign promises.

Typical of the media spin, a *U.S. News & World Report* article—titled "A Little Self-Restraint"—urged Clinton to stand tough against the demands of urban mayors or be labeled "a free-spending liberal."

During the dozen Reagan-Bush years, numerous mayors had demanded restoration of federal aid to cities. After Clinton's election, however, many of the same mayors piped down.

Five months into the Clinton term, *Newsweek* noted the new administration's message to the mayors. "The futility of complaint has become obvious: there will be no significant help for them from Washington, not even from a president who understands their problems…[and] probably couldn't have been elected without their support."

The Democrat who headed the National League of Cities in 1993, Donald Fraser (mayor of Minneapolis at the time), was willing to swallow the disappointment and make excuses: "We're getting more understanding of our problems and greater willingness to help from the Clinton administration. But they are severely constrained by the budget deficit they inherited."

Somehow, that deficit hasn't prevented the same administration's huge outlays for the Pentagon, three-quarters of a billion dollars each day. It all comes down to *priorities*. And inner-city residents—mostly black and Latino—aren't.

Our cities, and millions of people living in them, continue to suffer the consequences.

June 22, 1994

Media to Immigrants:
We Dim the Lamp for You

"Give me your tired, your poor, your huddled masses yearning to breathe free...I lift my lamp beside the golden door!" The inscription is engraved on the Statue of Liberty. But these days, a very different mood dominates the United States.

Much of the blame—or credit, depending on your point of view—should go to the mass media.

Few media voices are as blatantly anti-immigrant as some of the talk radio shouters. On WABC in New York, for example, Bob Grant has expressed hope that Haitian refugees would be left to drown: "Then they would stop coming in."

But even mainstream media debates begin with the premise that immigrants are a problem, and then focus narrowly on "controlling our borders" and "ending political asylum scams." In these discussions, advocates for immigrants and political refugees are often marginalized.

Also pushed to the sidelines are basic facts:

HISTORY: Except for the African-Americans whose ancestors arrived in chains and Native Americans who were here millennia ago, most of us are immigrants or descendants of immigrants who begged, borrowed or stole to get here. We arrived with or without legal documents, often fleeing persecution or deprivation. More media attention to this history might reveal the unseemliness of slamming Lady Liberty's "golden door" in the face of new immigrants.

ECONOMICS: You wouldn't know it from most media coverage, but immigrants—whether legal or illegal—benefit the U.S. economy, according to studies gathered by the Reagan and Bush administrations. Immigrants spur investment and job creation, work hard at often-unwanted jobs, and pay more in taxes than they take out in government services.

An exceptional *Business Week* cover story in July 1992, "Immigrants: How They're Helping the Economy," reported that "immigrants pay an estimated $90 billion in taxes, compared with the $5 billion in welfare benefits they receive." States with heavy immigration do carry increased school, health and welfare costs, but it's not because immigrants are ripping off the system. The problem is that the federal government doesn't share its windfall of immigrant taxes with the states most impacted.

"ILLEGALS": The overwhelming majority of immigrants and refugees—825,000 people per year—are admitted to the U.S. legally in a regulated, orderly fashion. The Census Bureau estimates that 200,000 to 300,000 enter illegally with the intent to take up residence. In other words, close to eight of ten immigrants are "legal." Only about 1.5 percent of our population is here without documents—and they are the ones least likely to use government services.

REFUGEES: Those who question our historic role as a beacon to political refugees suggest that the U.S. can't keep shouldering the world's problems. Of the 17 million refugees in the world today, less than 1 percent of them have been admitted to the United States. Based on their relative population size, Sweden, Canada and Australia resettle more political refugees than the U.S. does. Iran provides protection to millions of homeless Afghanis.

ETHNIC BIAS: Anti-immigrant feeling has long been driven by racial or ethnic prejudice. Ben Franklin looked down on the Germans coming to Pennsylvania. The "Know-Nothing" movement of the mid-1800s feared Catholic immigrants. Discriminatory laws sought to exclude Asians in the 1890s, and Southern and Eastern European immigrants in the 1920s.

Given how racially-charged the issue is, journalists should be alert to racist undertones in debates of immigration policy.

No organization on either side of the debate gets more

media exposure than the Federation for American Immigration Reform ("FAIR"—not to be confused with the media watch group). The Federation's leaders, who often appear without opposition in national news forums, sometimes play on racial stereotypes in calling for restricted immigration.

Responding to a reporter's question about the birthrates of Asian and Latino immigrants, Federation director Dan Stein remarked: "It's almost like they're getting into competitive breeding." The group's founder, John Tanton, covered the same ground in a memo: "Perhaps this is the first instance in which those with their pants up are going to get caught by those with their pants down." Tanton asked in the memo: "As whites see their power and control over their lives declining, will they simply go quietly into the night?"

Despite the heavy use of the Federation as a news source, U.S. media outlets have shown little curiosity about the group's financial support from the Pioneer Fund—described in the London *Sunday Telegraph* as a "neo-Nazi organization closely integrated with the far Right in American politics." From 1982 through last year, Pioneer has donated over a million dollars to the Federation, according to IRS records.

Founded in 1937 by textile manufacturer Wickliffe Draper, who favored sending blacks back to Africa, the Pioneer Fund's charter states that it is "committed to the proposition that people of different ethnic and cultural backgrounds are, on the basis of their heredity, inherently unequal and can never be expected to behave or perform equally."

In recent years, Pioneer has backed a grab bag of racist projects, including a neo-Nazi publication in Virginia linked to former genetic experimenters in Nazi Germany; a study at the University of Western Ontario, comparing brain size, penis size and IQ distribution among blacks, whites and Asians; and research by City College of New York professor Michael Levin, who claims that blacks as a group are less intelligent.

When our associate Steve Rendall interviewed Federation director Stein, he responded that Pioneer's support represented only a "small portion of our income," and quipped that "maybe it's better that Pioneer give its money to" his organization than to overt racists and fascists.

Whether today's immigrants are Mexicans, Chinese, Haitians or others, they're still "yearning to breathe free." News outlets should shed light on anti-immigrant prejudices—and the forces behind them.

August 4, 1993

Disabled People Face Media Obstacles

When disabled people are in the picture, the media focus is apt to be on the unusual.

So, on May 16 [1994], NBC News aired a TV report about "frivolous lawsuits and expensive hassles" stemming from the landmark Americans With Disabilities Act, signed into law four years earlier.

Introduced by Tom Brokaw as a segment "on good intentions and unintended consequences," the report acknowledged that the Act has improved the lives of many Americans. But that's not what the segment was about. It focused on the atypical—such as a dispute over making the highest ski slopes in California's Squaw Valley wheelchair accessible.

Unidentified "insiders," NBC declared, "have begun to question the cost of accommodating everyone who claims special status under the law."

To Greg Smith, sitting in his wheelchair in Phoenix, the network's spin was "quite unfair," he told us. While NBC concentrated on what Smith called the Act's "extreme applications," there was no mention of the "vast majority of instances where the law needs to be applied and nothing is happening."

Many businesses "are waiting until a complaint is filed to begin complying with the Americans With Disabilities Act." But, "thanks to NBC, many Americans now feel like the law is ridiculous."

A 30-year-old who has had muscular dystrophy since he was a child, Smith counts himself as part of a growing "disability awareness movement"—a movement "that is fueling itself even without media coverage."

For a year and a half now, he has hosted *On a Roll*—a call-in radio program in Arizona, introduced as "America's only weekly radio talk show on disability issues, civil rights and independent living. We're waging war on isolation, barriers and misconceptions."

A program addressed to a small minority? Hardly. In the United States, 48.9 million people have some form of disability, according to the President's Committee on Employment of People with Disabilities. Its report issued in March 1994 says that 14.7 million Americans of working age have a "severe disability."

Rather than exploring the day-to-day barriers that unnecessarily limit people with disabilities, many news stories have concentrated on unusual incidents like the ski-slope conflict.

Even efforts to meet the everyday needs of millions of disabled people are sometimes depicted as unreasonable.

In the midst of a battle over making Manhattan's public toilets usable for people in wheelchairs, the *New York Times* editorialized that "groups representing the disabled need to see the folly of clinging to unrealistic hopes that obstruct public needs." A *Wall Street Journal* editorial bemoaned "pressure from purported advocates for the disabled."

Another popular media theme is the courageous individual who overcomes handicaps with an indomitable spirit.

"Like stories of women who excelled at baking contests or blacks who were credits to their race, 'cripple stories' have for decades provided the only glimpses many Americans have had of the lives of people with disabilities," says Mary Johnson, former editor of the national newspaper *Disability Rag*.

The message, Johnson points out, is that "plucky disabled people who are heroic can overcome just about anything. Such sugar-coated stories have received play at the expense of news stories about conditions disabled people face in this country."

Those conditions include "rampant job discrimination," the "widespread failure of local and state governments to enforce laws requiring new buildings to be accessible," and "the failure of Medicare or Medicaid to support disabled people who want to stay out of nursing homes."

Johnson also sees a journalistic obstacle: "Those reporters who do perceive disability rights as an ongoing, newsworthy issue get hassled by editors bored with the whole concept."

Greg Smith, who produces and hosts *On a Roll* for KFNN

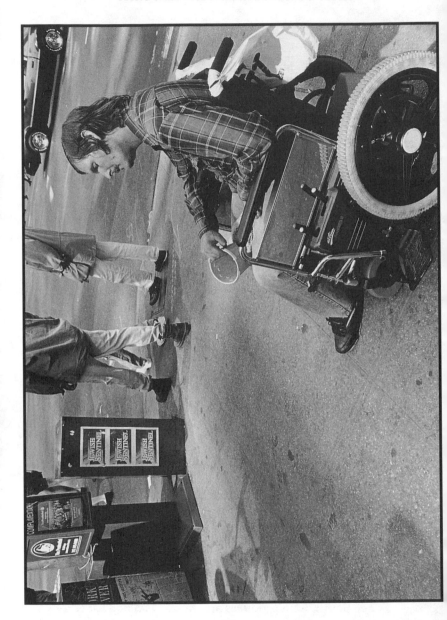

Radio in Phoenix, thinks that media coverage would be much better if it weren't for the bias that keeps disabled people out of many newsrooms.

"The news media should employ people who live the life and understand the issues," he says.

As a former radio sportscaster, Smith contends that media can no better report on disability issues without disabled people than cover sports without drawing on the insights of athletes.

"Emerging assistive technologies, the Americans With Disabilities Act, a new disability awareness movement and changing attitudes will make life more productive and enjoyable. But will people who hold management positions in the media recognize that it is in their own best interests to cover it? The best way to cover it is to hire people from within it who understand it."

Smith adds: "As an African-American with a severe disability, I have faced discrimination every day of my life…. However, devaluation as a result of my disability has been a greater limiting factor for me than racial discrimination. People's attitudes toward my disability have been the most difficult to overcome—more disabling than my muscular dystrophy."

Although Smith is upbeat—on and off the air—about what the future holds for disabled people, some broadcasters have told him that the topic is "too depressing" to merit a regular show.

The Corporation for Public Broadcasting has twice turned down an application for funds to offer *On a Roll* to public radio stations across the nation—despite the fact that so many millions of Americans are disabled.

"That's a huge potential audience," says Greg Smith, who's now working to syndicate the show on commercial radio. "You'd think broadcasters would embrace that large segment of the population." Unfortunately, the "stigma against disabled people" gets in the way.

May 18, 1994

Journalists Opening the Closet Door

Columnists often hope that their work will change other people's lives. Two years ago, Juan R. Palomo wrote a column that changed his own.

As a columnist for the *Houston Post*, Palomo sometimes shared information about himself. Once in a while he wrote about family or friends. But he had always carefully avoided letting on that he was gay.

Back in 1987, working as a reporter at the newspaper's bureau in Washington, D.C., he'd been "so in the closet" that he was afraid to suggest the paper assign a reporter to cover a national gay rights march there. He didn't, and it didn't.

But when a Houston man died at the hands of gay-bashers over the July 4th weekend in 1991, Palomo—in his ninth month of writing a three-times-a-week column—decided to leave the closet forever. He turned in a column denouncing anti-gay violence, and identifying himself as gay. In response, editors refused to print the article until he revised it to omit any reference to his own sexual orientation.

A city weekly got wind of the incident and called Palomo, who acknowledged what had occurred. When Palomo declined to promise that he would never again talk publicly about what had happened, he was fired—by a newspaper that had employed him as a journalist for a dozen years.

But that was not the end of the story. Most of the *Houston Post*'s reporters and editors signed a petition calling for his reinstatement. Gay and Latino activists denounced the firing. Subscribers phoned and wrote the paper in protest. A picket line went up. National publicity ensued. In the face of the uproar, the newspaper re-hired Juan Palomo.

Why is it important for gay and lesbian journalists to be open about their sexual orientation? For one thing, surveys consistently show that anti-gay hostility is far greater among those heterosexuals who live under the illusion that they don't know any gay males or lesbians.

"A recent *New York Times* poll revealed that an over-whelming majority of those who said they know someone who is homosexual have a more accepting view of us," Palomo points out. "That is why it's crucial that all of us stop hiding in the cold comfort of the closet."

When we spoke with Palomo a few days ago, he was emphatic about urging journalists to forsake that "cold com-fort" and take the risks of openness. "The action of coming out educates your co-workers," he said. And when that education takes place in newsrooms, it reverberates to the benefit of media consumers.

In Palomo's words, "People are anti-gay because they are ignorant. People fear what they do not know and do not under-stand... There are a lot of people who have a rigid stereotype of homosexuals. It's important for people to know that homo-sexuals do all kinds of work." Openly gay and lesbian and bisexual journalists "help to spread the word that we indeed are everywhere."

During the past couple of years, journalists at many news organizations have come out. Several hundred have joined the two-year-old National Lesbian and Gay Journalists Association.

"I'm happy to see a TV reporter who is free to sing with the gay-associated Seattle Men's Chorus in his off hours and also do all kinds of stories, not just stories on gay men," says writer Abba Solomon (a brother of one of us), who reviews for the *Northwest Gay and Lesbian Reader*.

Regular columns by open homosexuals are now being published in several big-city dailies including the *Philadelphia Inquirer*. Last summer a column covering "life from a gay per-spective"—by Deb Price, a lesbian writer for the *Detroit News*—went into national syndication, and now appears in about 20 papers.

"Being in the closet is a real mistake for a journalist," Price contends. "It's an asset for a newspaper to have openly gay journalists in the same way that having African-Americans or Hispanics or people with disabilities is an asset."

What's clear is that sexual orientation tells us nothing

about the content of someone's character or the integrity of someone's work.

The burden of challenging the straight-and-narrow of newsrooms, and creating workplaces that dispel stereotypes, should not fall only on gay and lesbian journalists.

If journalists—and readers—of all sexual orientations had not taken up that burden a couple of years ago, Juan Palomo would not be writing columns for the *Houston Post* today.

April 28, 1993

Part VIII
Labor in the Margins

In media coverage of economic life, Americans who do the bulk of the country's work are usually depicted as dry statistics rather than real live people. The assumption seems to be that members of the labor force have little to say worth hearing.

Cesar Chavez Obituaries
Bury Media Hypocrisy

In the two weeks since renowned labor leader Cesar Chavez died, we've accumulated over a dozen obituaries from major news outlets.

The obituaries are infuriating.

They aren't maddening because of inaccuracies. Indeed, the inspiring story is recounted in factual detail: How Chavez's grandparents immigrated to the U.S. from Mexico. How his parents built up a farm in Arizona but lost it during the Depression, and became migrant farm workers. How young Cesar never completed high school, but once recalled 65 elementary schools that he'd attended "for a day, a week or a few months."

As an adult, Chavez made history by successfully organizing largely immigrant, migratory farm workers—among the country's most exploited employees—into a union. His tactics borrowed from Gandhi and Martin Luther King: fasting, long marches, boycotts. He was a fearless giant at 5 feet 6 inches tall, a union president whose $5,000 salary equalled that of a farm laborer, a nonviolent leader who bowed down to no one.

So why complain about news accounts that dramatically and accurately reflect this great American life? The issue is hypocrisy.

All the glowing words that poured forth after Chavez's death stand in stark contrast to the many years of under-coverage of the people Chavez gave his life for—the workers in the fields and processing plants.

In the obits, Chavez was a "champion," a "legend," a "hero." But there is nothing heroic about news outlets that have routinely dodged the issue of exploited farm laborers.

In his obituary of Chavez, ABC anchor Peter Jennings referred to farm workers and "their pitiful wages and sometimes deplorable working conditions." Our computer search of

ABC World News Tonight stories focusing on the deplorable conditions of U.S. farm workers turned up only one segment in the last 40 months.

CNN ran lengthy reports on the death of Cesar Chavez, referring to farm workers as the "most politically and socially disadvantaged." The network could have added *media disadvantaged.* Since Jan. 1, 1990, CNN has aired only a half-dozen reports exploring the conditions of these disadvantaged; the 480-word Chavez obituary was longer than almost all of them.

The kind words about the departed hero may make reporters and TV anchors feel good, but they do nothing for the workers in the fields. What would do a lot for them is solid reporting.

It would help if media prominently, and regularly, reported that workers in the fields suffer more job-related illness than in any other industry. Several times more. And farm labor is getting more dangerous; each year, pesticide exposure affects about 300,000 workers. For most farm laborers, the low pay is accompanied by no health coverage or disability plans, no pay for sick days or overtime.

Reporting some history would also be helpful in showing the political roots of today's appalling conditions. Most Americans probably don't know that when Congress passed the landmark Wagner Act in the 1930s, sanctioning the right of workers to form unions and bargain collectively with employers, agribusiness interests lobbied successfully to exclude any protections for farm workers.

In California, the advent of Cesar Chavez and the United Farm Workers of America (UFW) in the 1960s, and passage of the state's Agricultural Labor Relations Act in 1975, significantly improved wages and conditions for farm workers.

But when union-ally Jerry Brown left the governor's office and was replaced by a friend of agribusiness, the state law—which required "good faith" bargaining—became a joke. Workers on hundreds of farms democratically elected the UFW to represent them, but employers simply refused to bargain—and faced absolutely no sanctions from the state.

This history is hardly debatable. It's also hardly reported. If mass media toughly scrutinized the corporations responsible for the plight of farm workers, they'd be targeting some of their biggest advertisers: produce companies, wineries, supermarket chains.

Our media culture worships celebrities, and likes to believe in David versus Goliath sagas. Since Goliath owns the big media, the death of Cesar Chavez is a perfect, and harmless, story. Journalists can show their kinship with the downtrodden and feel good about themselves as they tell the story of a real-life David, now deceased.

Not as easy for mass media to tell is why the conditions of farm workers in our country remain so abysmal. Such reporting might offend powerful interests. Goliaths would be exposed.

So when the charismatic leader of the farm workers dies, that's big news. But when his followers die due to pesticides, lousy health care and unsafe working conditions, that's not big news.

It's infuriating.

May 5, 1993

Life in the Margins for U.S. Workers

It's a good thing Labor Day was established. Otherwise, a whole year might pass at some news outlets with hardly any acknowledgement that workers exist.

It sometimes takes an alert news consumer to spot items about labor. On July 26 [1993], for example, a front page *New York Times* report on how the Midwest flood was hurting railroad commerce contained this throwaway remark: "The strikes hobbling Eastern coal production appear to be a more important factor than the flooding."

The remark must have surprised readers unaware that strikes were indeed "hobbling Eastern coal production." The strikes, which began in West Virginia in May and expanded to 18,000 workers in eight states, had never made the *New York Times* front page before.

A few weeks ago, the national edition of the *Times* carried the page-one headline, "Kodak Will Cut 10,000 Jobs; Further Hard Choices Likely." The "hard choices" were those of Kodak's managers. Their statements—along with those of Wall Street analysts—dominated the Aug. 19 [1993] article. But Kodak workers were invisible in the story; not a single affected employee was quoted.

For years now, news about workers has been shrinking in mainstream media. Many dailies no longer have labor reporters—which leads not only to less coverage, but less informed coverage. The *Wall Street Journal* assigned a reporter to cover the United Mine Workers who'd never heard of the legendary leader of that union, John L. Lewis.

When coverage of U.S. workers shrinks, it may seem to be a natural process. After all, industries that were once big news are now declining; so is union membership.

But in fact, the process is unnatural...and biased. Most Americans—whether in a union or not—work for a salary or wage. Millions of us are interested in issues like job security and safety, fair treatment by management, family leave, benefits, pensions.

So there's nothing natural or neutral going on when CNN or PBS chooses to offer various regular programs looking at corporate and investment issues, but not a single show devoted to workers' issues.

Nor is there anything natural about newspapers that have daily business sections, but no labor pages.

Newspapers do report on workplace issues in the business section, but such coverage is often biased. During his years covering the labor beat for the *Chicago Tribune*, James Warren insisted on not being linked to the business desk. His reason? "Business editors have a skewed view on labor stories and the business section tends to be a bulletin board for corporate America."

William Serrin covered work and labor for the *New York Times* until 1986. "I had the curious idea that you have to put workers in the paper like you put corporate executives in the paper," he recalled. "I was suspect. And the more good stories I wrote, the harder I did my job, the more suspect I was."

When Serrin submitted stories, like a profile of a steel worker, editors would sometimes react: "Bill, you're too pro-worker."

"Pro-worker" sympathies of a reporter are subject to question, but who challenges pro-business bias? A *Los Angeles Times* poll revealed that in labor-management disputes, 53 percent of newspaper editors said they generally sided with management, while only 8 percent sided with labor.

Perhaps this explains why strike coverage often focuses more on how the strike is hurting consumers than on the issues rankling the workers. During the short-lived railroad strike in 1992, newspapers accused the rarely quoted workers—who'd been without a contract or a raise for years—of everything from causing "commuter chaos" to threatening the country's "economic recovery."

With so much ink devoted to the negative impact on consumers, you'd think the union was on strike against them rather than management. Yet buried at the end of one article was the acknowledgement that "most train riders expressed support for the striking workers."

In 1989, researcher Jonathan Tasini tallied a year's worth of reporting on workers' issues—including child care, minimum wage and workplace safety—aired on the CBS, NBC and ABC evening news. It amounted to only 2.3 percent of total news coverage.

The survey found that if it weren't for a bitter strike at Eastern Airlines, coverage of U.S. unions would have been "undetectable." Coal miners got far more and better coverage on American TV if they went on strike in the Soviet Union than in Virginia. Eight days of a Soviet coal strike received 37 minutes of coverage. An extraordinary nine-month strike by U.S. miners against the Pittston Company—which included the takeover of a coal plant—received only 23 minutes.

The most shocking statistic in the survey was the lack of coverage of workplace safety—a total of only 13 minutes on the three networks for the entire year. More than at any time since the era of sweatshops, U.S. workers are being injured and killed on the job—many due to carcinogens not in use before World War II. Yet in all of 1989, workplace safety warranted a total of 40 seconds on *NBC Nightly News*. NBC's corporate parent, General Electric, which has an appalling work safety record, benefits from such noncoverage.

Job safety is just one of many dramatic workplace stories being undercovered today. You've heard something about U.S. jobs being exported to Mexico for cheaper, less protected labor, but little about the efforts of some U.S. unions to link up with Mexican unions to protect those workers.

Another underreported story is the growing resentment felt by labor activists who dislike the AFL-CIO's submissive stance toward the Clinton White House. To hear this administration talk today, unions may be outdated. Labor Secretary Robert Reich told a *New York Times* reporter: "The jury is still out on whether the traditional union is necessary for the new workplace." Commerce Secretary Ron Brown makes similar comments.

The Clinton administration—whose cabinet may be the wealthiest in history—often displays little patience for unions and workers' concerns.

Wealthy media outlets often show the same disinterest. Flowery rhetoric on Labor Day cannot undo that reality.

September 1, 1993

TOM TOMORROW ©12-7-93 ...WITH APOLOGIES TO MIKE JUDGE...

Labor Day Is a Reminder
of the Forgotten

When Labor Day comes around, we hear some nice things about working people. And then, at most news outlets, it's back to business as usual—paying little attention to labor issues.

National media seem to have an unwritten rule: If a labor-management conflict isn't disrupting big-league sports or transportation, it isn't very important.

For seven years, researcher Andrew Tyndall has kept track of the nightly TV news programs on the ABC, CBS and NBC networks. His figures show that if you go on strike and you aren't a pro athlete or an airline employee, your national news value is close to zero.

In August [1994], the baseball strike received far more network TV news coverage than any other labor event of the 1990s. Since 1987, nine of the top ten stories on strikes have involved major-league baseball and football players, airline machinists, flight attendants and railroad employees.

The only exception came during the bitter strike pitting the United Auto Workers against Caterpillar, which manufactures earth-moving equipment. National coverage peaked in spring 1992. But the battle, centered in Illinois, has raged on.

In June [1994], more than 13,000 UAW workers went on strike after Caterpillar refused to discuss allegations of nearly 100 specific unfair labor practices, such as the firing of 11 workers for union activity.

Outside the glare of network TV lights, the heartland city of Decatur, Illinois, has become "strike town"—many workers call it "the war zone"—with thousands of industrial employees on picket lines at three different targets: Caterpillar, the A.E. Staley paper-processing plant and the Bridgestone/Firestone tire company.

More than 700 Staley workers have been locked out of their jobs for more than a year—since management demanded

12-hour shifts and other changes. At Firestone, the issues include 12-hour shifts, elimination of cost-of-living adjustments, and cutbacks in health coverage.

Many other labor disputes have been simmering around the country—some for a very long time.

In Stockton, California, 550 cannery workers—mostly women of Mexican, African or Asian descent—are now entering the *fourth year* of a strike against Diamond Walnut. Teamsters Union official Barbara Christe said in an interview that it took two and a half years before media outside the region began to report on the strike.

Back in 1985, Diamond Walnut workers (earning between $5 and $10 per hour) accepted pay cuts of 35 percent—with the agreement that their wages would return to normal once the company returned to financial health. But in 1991, after posting large profits, the company offered only a ten-cents-an-hour wage increase while insisting on a new setback for employees: $33 a month in health insurance co-payments.

When workers went out on strike, the company hired permanent "striker replacements." In response, longtime employees—many of them single mothers—have been picketing, rallying, fasting and urging a consumer boycott of Diamond Walnuts.

Across the United States, permanent replacement of striking workers—a practice outlawed in other industrialized countries—has undermined the bargaining power of American unions. A *Washington Post* editorial applauded when a Senate filibuster in July [1994] blocked passage of a House-approved measure to prohibit the hiring of "permanent replacements" during strikes.

"Overall, labor gets lousy coverage," said Christe, still hard at work in support of the Diamond Walnut strikers. "The newspaper owners have decided to do away with the labor beat. There's definitely a business bias." Newspaper coverage of labor is now commonly left to the business section.

For three decades, until his retirement a couple of years ago, Harry Bernstein was a labor reporter for the *Los Angeles*

Times. When Bernstein started in 1962, about 35 percent of the U.S. work force was unionized; today that figure is at 15 percent. "I think that the editors of the newspapers made the decision that unions were not as important as they once were," he told us, "and that pushed the unions down further."

If the public had a thorough understanding of unions, Bernstein said, "there would be more support for them."

Those hoping for better coverage of workers on "public television" have been disappointed, as independent Rep. Bernie Sanders of Vermont—the only member of Congress who is neither a Democrat nor a Republican—pointed out on the floor of the House of Representatives recently.

"It is…not an accident," Sanders said, "that on commercial radio and television there is very little serious discussion about the enormous problems facing the working people and the poor of this nation. The average working family in America is in trouble…. But that reality is not reflected in the corporately controlled media."

"Year after year," Sanders added, "it appears that public television is more and more coming to resemble commercial television. I do not object that there are three regularly scheduled business shows on PBS—*Wall $treet Week*, the *Nightly Business Report* and *Adam Smith's Money World*. I have no problem with those programs. I do have a problem, however, that there is not one regularly scheduled program on PBS…reflecting the interests of working people and organized labor."

But all is not bleak. A feisty show about the American workplace, *We Do The Work*, airs on 70 public TV stations—even though it gets no support from PBS at the national level. The good news is that *We Do The Work* has just gone into more frequent production; it's now a weekly program. For labor, a bright spot on a grim media landscape.

August 31, 1994

Unreported and Poignant, the Human Voices of Labor Strife

DECATUR, Ill.—Watching thousands of American workers march through this community that has become a labor battleground, it's painful to remember that they are nearly invisible on the national media map.

After many years of punching clocks at the A.E. Staley paper plant or the Bridgestone/Firestone tire factory or the Caterpillar machinery complex, more than a third of this city's manufacturing work force is on strike or locked out of their jobs.

Today, on a sunny Saturday afternoon in mid-October [1994], workers walk a dozen abreast—past barbed fences where they used to report for work—chanting "Solidarity." And: "Injury to one, injury to all."

Some are close to retirement age. Others, still young, stride hand-in-hand with small children.

What they have to say won't reach very far beyond the march route. Few TV viewers or news readers will catch a glimpse of their anger and determined dignity—the kind of dignity found among people fighting to defend their homes and families.

And there is little chance that news reports will convey the messages they're carrying. The most common one says, in big block letters: "CORPORATE GREED IS TEARING DECATUR APART."

Another sign, in hundreds of hands, includes photos of magnates who run Staley and Firestone and Caterpillar, with the words: "STOP THESE THUGS!" Another sign: "Punish Corporate Criminals, *Not* Their Victims."

Almost everyone is wearing inscribed shirts.

"AMERICA: Union Built, by blood, labor, sweat."

"Illegally Terminated by CAT."

"We'll *never* forget Labor War of '94."

"CAT can't break our solidarity."

"Don't ever give up!"

And, on the back of a shirt worn by a man with many lines in his face, a silkscreened quote from a United Auto Workers leader: "The fight…is more than a dispute over a labor agreement. It is a fight for our basic right as workers and as citizens."

The banners are also a poor bet for the news:

"The Labor Movement—We brought you the weekend!"

"Labor Creates All Wealth."

Marchers move onto a viaduct over the ghostly gray-white Staley plant, where management suddenly locked out 760 union members 16 months ago. A big new sign hangs on one of the buildings: "STALEY DECATUR—Rededicated to EXCELLENCE."

The workers see Staley policies differently: replacing eight-hour days with 12-hour shifts and eliminating overtime pay, plus rollbacks of key health provisions, safety protections and the right to grievance.

Along Decatur's 22nd Street, the march passes fenced rows of long three-story brick buildings—the Firestone plant. Up ahead is Decatur's Caterpillar factory. The mood is somber.

When a van from a local TV station, WAND, arrives on the scene and a young reporter emerges from the vehicle, his appearance sets off a negative buzz. Some marchers start yelling at him: "W-CAT! W-CAT!"

The TV reporter takes it as an insult. The relationship between strikers and local media is "a strained one," Sean Streaty says, sounding puzzled. "We try to be as neutral as we can," he adds, but "they feel it [news coverage] is biased."

It's not only in Decatur that Cat workers are on strike. Charging the company with unfair labor practices, more than 10,000 employees at various sites have been out since the first day of summer.

One Cat striker who drove in from Peoria for this demonstration, Billye Reed, doesn't hesitate when we ask what's at stake: "They're just trying to break our union. That's what it boils down to."

Reed, who's 51, speaks with quiet rage, and a bit of bewilderment. She has worked 20 years for Caterpillar, a company that posted sales of $2.9 billion and profits of well over $100 mil-

Solidarity march crosses Decatur's 22nd Street viaduct, Oct. 15, 1994.

Police spray workers with pepper gas at Staley plant gates, Decatur, June 25, 1994.

lion last year. These days, top managers seem indifferent, even hostile, to her future.

"They call it 'plant modernization.' What it boils down to is eliminating people's jobs." She pauses, her brown curly hair almost reaching the shoulders of her United Auto Workers jacket. "If they eliminate my job, where am I going to look for work?"

Imagine your mother, or sister, or daughter, asking such a question at age 51.

"If we lose this battle, our retirement's gone," she adds. "They don't think about the workers who've given their lives to the company."

Then she looks wistful. "I don't understand why they don't have a conscience. That's what I don't understand."

A few miles away, a couple of men outside the Firestone dealership on Main Street are taking care of a routine chore—picketing the store. They've been on strike since mid-July.

Cecil Peveler has worked at the Bridgestone/Firestone plant for 13 years. Now, the company's insistence on 12-hour shifts is a threat to precious time with his children. "That's going to take me away from my family life as far as watching my kids grow up. Volleyball games, baseball, basketball, track—all those things are activities that take place in evening hours. If you're working you can't go."

A picket sign in his hand, a "Stop Scabs" button pinned to his shirt, an American Flag decal on his shoulder, Peveler stands next to his picketing partner. Reggie Merrill is also in his early forties, also with more than a dozen years at Bridgestone/Firestone.

Merrill speaks of a decline in real wages, an erosion of vacations. "We do not want anything more," he says. "We just want to keep what we have."

In the mass media, we hear little from people on the labor frontlines, people like Billye Reed, Cecil Peveler, Reggie Merrill. They have much to say. Many people would like to listen. But workers don't own big media institutions.

October 19, 1994

Part IX
Clinton Priorities on
the Home Front

Starting off with orchestrated strains of Camelot and persistent advice from the fourth estate, the Clinton administration pledged to "put people first." But in the political dance that followed, the president (and the media) promoted other agendas.

Washington's Status Quo Hurts Taxpayers: No Big Story

With the April 15th tax deadline nearing [in 1993], it's a good time to consider a proverb that could have been coined in Washington: *The more things change, the more they stay the same.*

Since the advent of the Clinton administration, some things have changed significantly—such as abortion policy, and the dawning of a debate on gays in the military.

But many things have stayed the same. For example: The same people and institutions that shaped key financial policy through the disastrous 1980s are still determining policy today. Taxpayers smarting from the savings and loan bailout might be curious to know how little has changed.

Big news story? Not really. What stays the same in Washington—business as usual—is often overlooked by the national press corps. The control of fiscal policies by old line banking and Wall Street interests is an old story. Ho-hum.

Editors may see these as unremarkable "dog bites man" stories, but the public might appreciate more rigorous media scrutiny of the pedigreed officials who are taking a big bite out of taxpayer wallets.

Let's start with Lloyd Bentsen.

Testifying before the House Banking Committee a few weeks ago, Treasury Secretary Bentsen asked for another $45 billion toward the cleanup of savings and loans. Most of the money would go to the notorious RTC (Resolution Trust Corporation)—which could stand for "Reward The Crooks"—the agency that takes over failed S&Ls and liquidates their assets.

Though he now visits Capitol Hill as a White House emissary, for years Bentsen headed the Senate Finance Committee, befriended the banking and insurance lobbies, and helped give away the store during the 1980s. As a senator, Bentsen was an ally of Reaganite tax and deregulation policies that Bill Clinton denounced throughout the 1992 campaign as "trickle-down economics."

Four years earlier, during campaign '88, two words explained why the Democratic presidential ticket couldn't use the S&L issue against the Republicans—Lloyd Bentsen. The vice-presidential candidate warned Michael Dukakis to avoid the issue because of Bentsen's own connections to it.

Bentsen's role is explored in a new book by former *Houston Post* reporter Pete Brewton—which blames Washington policy and deregulation for making many S&Ls vulnerable to looting by unscrupulous individuals, some of whom were mobsters and CIA operators. Businessman/politician Lloyd Bentsen himself sold an S&L to people with ties to organized crime, who proceeded to loot the till.

The title of Brewton's book is *The Mafia, the CIA and George Bush: The Untold Story of America's Greatest Financial Debacle.* In the introduction, the author calls the savings and loan fiasco "a bipartisan scandal," pointing out that if the Democrats had won the 1988 election, Brewton's book would have been titled: *The Mafia, the CIA and Lloyd Bentsen.*

Like George Bush's clan, Lloyd Bentsen's family was heavily involved in the S&L mess. If you inspected the fine print of your newspaper March 30 [1993], you might have seen a short wire story about his son: Real estate investor Lan Bentsen agreed to pay $28 million of the "$54 million owed by ventures he controls to the Resolution Trust Corporation, the federal agency that cleans up failed savings and loans." That's Lan Bentsen making an agreement with the federal agency his dad is in charge of.

But the problem goes deeper. Lloyd Bentsen just appointed an assistant to oversee the RTC who is no stranger to the S&L bailout. Deputy Treasury Secretary Roger C. Altman came to Washington from his leadership post at the Blackstone Group, a Wall Street firm which profited from its dealings with the RTC. [Altman was forced to resign in August 1994 after misleading Congress about Whitewater.]

And while we're naming those who help Clinton set policy, let's not forget his "chief economic adviser," Robert E. Rubin—a man whose financial disclosure statement shows earnings of about $30 million in 1992. Until January he headed the powerful Goldman, Sachs and Co., which contributed to Sen. Bentsen's campaign coffers. That firm has made a mint off the RTC and failed S&Ls.

As he was moving from Wall Street to Pennsylvania Avenue, Rubin sent a bizarre—and revealing—note to his corporate clients, saying: "I look forward to continuing to work with you in my new capacity."

Far from being cast out of the temples of power, the "trickle-down" patrons that Clinton denounced during the campaign are in the White House inner sanctum. An inside account in the *Wall Street Journal*, telling how Clinton and advisers hashed out the budget plan, reported on Bentsen's "superior status at the meetings." The president repeatedly turned to him and asked: "Lloyd, what would you do?"

As you head off toward some mailbox to dispatch this year's tax return, you might wonder why economic policy continues to be in the hands of the same millionaires who cleaned up in the 1980s.

And why continuation of the status quo is no big story.

[In December 1994, with Bentsen departing as treasury secretary, President Clinton chose Robert Rubin to replace him. "The change is expected to have little impact on policy," Associated Press reported matter-of-factly, "since both men are pro-business Democrats."]

April 7, 1993

Media Elite Prods Clinton
Toward Status Quo

For days after the selection of David Gergen to be a top White House adviser [in May 1993], the Washington press corps showered President Clinton's move with near-unanimous praise.

If we had real diversity in national media, tough questions would be widespread. For example: Is it hypocritical for a man who became president by denouncing 12 years of Reagan-Bush trickle-down economics to appoint Gergen, one of the most successful salesmen of Reaganomics?

But such blunt questions were rarely posed—even after Clinton proclaimed that the Gergen appointment "signals to the American people where I am, what I believe and what I'm going to do."

Far from being diverse or "liberal," the national media have functioned with remarkable uniformity in recent months, pressuring Clinton away from key campaign pledges. Bringing in a former Reagan media strategist was a symbolic white flag hoisted by the current White House—a gesture of surrender to an establishment press that has pounded at Clinton to avoid serious reform.

The *New York Times,* which has contributed to the pounding, headlined its report on the Gergen appointment: "An Offering To the Wolves."

The headline had unintended insight. Among the wolves of the media elite, anxiety over the intentions of the first Democratic president in a dozen years has been palpable. They've snarled and snapped at any indication the new man in the White House might actually carry out the populist promises that helped put him there.

On a daily basis during the summer and fall campaign, Clinton condemned policies that favor the rich over people of ordinary means. He attacked the Republicans as captives of corporate lobbyists and contributors. He promised to reform the tax structure, and to invest in job creation as a way of reducing the deficit. He pledged that his inclusionary politics would bring new faces to Washington.

The campaign paid off for Clinton—especially among women and racial minorities. If only white men had voted, George Bush would still be president.

But from the day Clinton was elected, leading political journalists—such as Steve Roberts of *U.S. News & World Report*—began instructing him on how to break his promises of change, including his pledges for campaign finance reform. A post-election *New York Times* report stated: "For a politician with as many promises as Mr. Clinton, keeping to a few priorities will require self-restraint."

Journalists are supposed to expose politicians who break promises—not encourage them, or hail them for "self-restraint."

Mass media also weighed in against Clinton when he sought to fulfill his pledge of looking beyond the Beltway to include fresh faces in his administration. A media furor greeted several such *outsider* candidates.

President Clinton's continual backpedaling on reform promises—military cuts, job stimulus, Haitian refugees, gays in the armed forces, etc.—has alienated key Democratic Party constituencies. Their leaders, whose views about the administration rarely appear in establishment media, say that White House waffling and indecisiveness are largely to blame for Clinton's drop in the polls.

But in recent weeks, many national news outlets have united in blaming Clinton's failures on one main factor: the "lurch to the left." Reports on this theme have ignored basic standards of balanced journalism—especially the requirement that people from various sides be quoted.

Typical was a "Clinton has veered left" news story in the *New York Times* a week before the Gergen appointment. Quoting only disgruntled conservative Democrats, the article offered an unrebutted compilation of dubious claims: That Clinton was elected because he campaigned as a conservative. (No evidence was cited.) That liberals dominate Clinton's cabinet—news that would surprise Treasury Secretary Lloyd Bentsen, Defense Secretary Les Aspin and others.

The story included the assertion that Clinton has "done everything Jesse Jackson could have asked for." *Times* reporter Michael Kelly didn't bother quoting Jackson or kindred spirits. If he had, that statement and the whole article would have been rendered absurd. When we called Jackson's office, we were provided a laundry list of (Jackson-supported) progressive measures which Clinton endorsed during the campaign, but abandoned after entering the White House.

Given the media drumbeat about Clinton's supposed "leftward lurch," perhaps it's no surprise that in selecting David Gergen, a compliant president spouted media catchphrases about purging his administration of "a tinge that is too partisan and not connected to the mainstream."

To those who voted for Bill Clinton because of his message of change, these words of contrition might sound disappointingly like "Return to the status quo."

New York Times columnist William Safire, who helped popularize the "lurch to the left" myth, used the Gergen appointment as an opportunity to gloat and declare victory. He concluded his May 31 column by exhorting Clinton to prove his compliance by recognizing that "taxpayer-subsidized health insurance does not fit into the mainstream."

As with most "leftward lurch" propaganda, there was a tiny problem: evidence. In poll after poll conducted by Safire's *New York Times*, majorities of the public endorse "tax-financed health insurance."

Fitting "into the mainstream"—as defined by Washington's media elite—means scorning programs that could benefit most Americans.

June 2, 1993

Clinton Looking Away
From Domestic Neglect

A week before his meeting with Asian government leaders in Seattle [November 1993], President Clinton delivered a passionate speech about inner-city crime. He bemoaned a "great crisis of the spirit that is gripping America today."

Clinton quoted Martin Luther King Jr., while giving short shrift to King's message of social justice. After ten months in the White House, the sad truth is that Bill Clinton has backtracked on his promises of economic renewal for the United States.

After reneging on his pledges to "invest in America," Clinton is pushing for the U.S. to get more of the economic action in the Pacific Rim—where many countries implemented smarter economic priorities long ago.

When Clinton was campaigning for the presidency, he vowed to boost federal spending for education, training, infrastructure, research and development. Yet the Fiscal Year 1994 federal budget—his first—is scarcely an improvement over recent years.

"In terms of public investment," says Todd Schafer of the D.C.-based Economic Policy Institute, "by all measures the Clinton administration has done little better than the Bush administration. By some measures it has done worse."

Inadequate public investment erodes wages. In the United States, real wages have been declining for two decades—down 16 percent, even while the real Gross Domestic Product has increased by more than half. Twenty years ago, U.S. manufacturing jobs were the highest compensated in the world. Now a dozen countries have surpassed us.

"The relative low level of public investment has had a major impact on U.S. productivity and competitiveness," Schafer points out. And the situation is not about to improve.

In Clinton's first annual budget, "investment has been sacrificed for the goal of deficit reduction," Schafer adds. "As a result, the share of the economy devoted to federal investment programs will be lower in Fiscal Year 1994 than in Fiscal Year 1993."

Soon after he was elected, Clinton abandoned his campaign call for a modest "stimulus package" for jobs and infrastructure repair. The package totalled a mere $30 billion, but that was too much for many media pundits, who urged Clinton to ditch the idea—and then cheered when he did so.

Clinton was even quicker to jettison his promise of federal assistance for U.S. cities. He never even submitted an urban aid program to Congress, even though our cities are literally falling apart.

While the president speaks of his concern for young Americans, Schafer observes, "we are neglecting the human, physical, and technological infrastructure upon which their economic future depends."

But that neglect didn't stop Clinton from going to Memphis in mid-November to preach about America's spiritual crisis from the same pulpit where Martin Luther King gave his last speech.The president recalled some of King's words— but not his observation that "a nation that continues year after year to spend more money on military defense than on programs of social uplift is approaching spiritual death.... The time has come for us to civilize ourselves by the total, direct and immediate abolition of poverty."

A quarter-century after King's death, abolishing poverty is not on the White House agenda. Clinton's budget invested little for military-to-civilian conversion. Indeed, U.S. government spending priorities are in sharp contrast with those of many Asian countries.

In the United States, during the 1980s, government investment in civilian physical infrastructure accounted for only 0.3 percent of Gross Domestic Product. In Japan, the figure was 5.7 percent. As Doug Henwood, editor of *Left Business Observer*, notes: "For our country to reach Japanese levels of public investment would require a boost of $324 billion in U.S. spending for infrastructure."

But President Clinton has no such intentions.

While the structure of U.S. economic life continues to erode, Clinton is fervently pitching for trade in Asia, and elsewhere. The tragedy is that the president is acceding to the continued neglect of our country's most precious resource—its people.

November 17, 1993

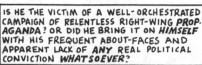

"Middle Class" Image Veils
Fat-Cats Behind Democrats

Few political groups have won such consistently favorable media treatment in recent years as the Democratic Leadership Council.

Founded in 1985 by Bill Clinton, Al Gore and other Southern Democrats as a pressure group within the national Democratic Party, the DLC pledged to move the party away from "special interests" and toward "the middle class." Since then, the DLC has gained enormous power and prestige.

But few journalists have bothered to report that the DLC is itself rife with "special interests."

Now, leaked DLC documents provide new evidence of corporate ties that bind the Clinton presidency and the Democratic Leadership Council.

A memo from the DLC's development director, dated March 7 [1994], clearly was not intended to see the light of day. It identifies specific DLC politicians—including the president and vice president of the United States—who would "be most successful in soliciting the contribution" from particular fat-cats for the DLC's political policy arm.

The memo suggests that President Clinton approach poultry tycoon Donald Tyson, of Tyson Foods, for a hefty contribution. In addition, it urges that Clinton target multibillionaire businessman Warren Buffett, the principal stockholder of the ABC/Cap Cities media conglomerate.

The memo also sets out a plan for Vice President Gore to seek funds for DLC operations from Disney cable executive John Cooke. Conveniently, Gore heads the Clinton administration's policy team on the information superhighway—with huge implications for Disney's cable investments.

A newsletter called *Counterpunch* (published by the Washington-based Institute for Policy Studies) obtained the DLC memo—later described by a DLC spokesperson as "an internal fundraising document."

One key question remains about the memo: *Did Clinton or Gore know about their behind-the-scenes fundraising roles spelled out in the memo?*

In the very first words of its May 30 [1994] news report on the existence of the DLC memo, the *Washington Post* cleared the nation's top two officials of any complicity: "President Clinton and Vice President Gore don't know it yet, but the Democratic Leadership Council…has listed them on internal memos as 'solicitors' to court wealthy people for a new DLC fundraising drive."

There's one problem with that statement. The *Post* reporter who wrote it, Charles Babcock, didn't know if it was true. And he still doesn't.

"I probably should have said *may* not know it," Babcock told us in a June 13 interview. The first ten words of his article, he said, were based on a "hunch."

Like the *Washington Post,* we were unable to get the White House to comment on when Clinton and Gore knew about the memo.

In any case, the scenario sketched out in the DLC memo signifies a new low in the DLC's tawdry activities. And that's low, indeed.

Year after year, DLC national meetings have been dominated by corporate lobbyists, many of them Republicans. At the DLC annual conference in March 1989, nearly 100 lobbyists subsidized the event by paying between $2,500 and $25,000 each. (In a moment of candor, DLC president Al From acknowledged: "There's no question you can define 'special interest' as our sponsors.")

The DLC's main thrust inside the Democratic Party has been to deride loyal activist constituencies—such as labor, racial minorities and feminists—as pushy *special interests.*

But the negative "special interests" tag is rarely affixed to the DLC and its big-money backers, including the top echelons of Arco, Prudential-Bache, Dow Chemical, Boeing, RJR Nabisco, Georgia Pacific, the Tobacco Institute, the American Petroleum

Institute and Martin Marietta.

The corporate heavies behind the Democratic Leadership Council wouldn't know a middle-class person if their limousines ran over one. Yet that hasn't stopped the DLC—and Clinton, who was hoisted to the national political stage by the DLC—from swearing dedication to "the middle class" almost daily.

President Clinton rang the trusty bell in a speech to the DLC six months ago: "We must be the party of the values and the interests of the middle class..." In late 1992, President-elect Clinton appeared at a DLC banquet in his honor, helping to raise $3 million for the group in a single night; as usual, middle class folks and "values" were hard to find at the DLC event—which cost $15,000 per plate.

The DLC has specialized in blaming the victims of chronic discrimination, instead of faulting conditions of unequal opportunity. "It's time to shift the primary focus from racism, the traditional enemy from without, to self-defeating patterns of behavior, the new enemy within," declared close Clinton ally and DLC stalwart Charles Robb, then governor of Virginia, in 1986.

Hailing that approach as evidence of new maturity among "New Democrats," the news media have routinely depicted the DLC as a force for sobriety within a party in recovery from liberal inebriation.

With typical hype, *Newsweek* senior editor Joe Klein once lauded the DLC as "the party's most intellectually adventurous group."

The fawning coverage of DLC-style Democrats by powerful media outlets may explain why some conservatives complain of "pro-Democrat" news bias. There's only one catch: These Democrats are more like Republicans.

"The DLC has largely won both the strategic fight over the importance of the middle class and the substantive fight over what values should be reflected in social programs," *Washington Post* journalist (and Clinton guru) E.J. Dionne Jr. wrote last December. In a telling observation, he added that the DLC hier-

archy's "most important White House ally is David Gergen"—
the former aide to President Reagan now handling media
strategy for President Clinton.

The sleaze that flows between high-rolling corporations
and high-placed politicians is bipartisan, and deserves much
more media scrutiny than it gets—especially when perpetuated
by political groups claiming to speak on behalf of "the middle
class."

June 15, 1994

Media Blind Spots:
Voting Blocs That Stayed Home

After two years of largely following the advice of media pundits, the Clinton administration and its allies took a drubbing on Election Day 1994.

It should surprise no one that by the time Nov. 8 rolled around, many black Americans lacked enthusiasm for the much-ballyhooed "New Democrats." So did a lot of union members, and the urban poor.

Only in the last days of the '94 campaign did reporters and pundits talk about the importance of the Democratic base, often referred to as the party's "traditional" constituencies. For the previous 103 weeks, since Bill Clinton won the presidency, journalists commonly depicted those old Democrats as impediments to the new White House team—irrelevant nuisances or "special interests."

These constituencies heard promises of "aid to urban America" and "investment in jobs" from the Clinton campaign in 1992; since then they have been mostly ignored—to the delight of many mainstream pundits.

With a low turnout among traditional Democrats facilitating major Republican triumphs, the vote totals summon up a sobering adage: *Be careful what you ask for; you might get it.*

At the urging of inside-the-Beltway media sages, the president has viewed habitual Democratic voters as peripheral to his political calculations. That mindset holds that poor people don't count for much. Neither do strong advocates for labor, or the environment, or civil rights. They're seen as special interests with more lung-power than clout.

To some extent, Bill Clinton courted those groups during the '92 campaign. But as president, his attentions have been focused elsewhere.

Just after winning the White House, the president-elect could read in the nation's biggest newsweekly, *Time*, that

"Clinton's willingness to move beyond some of the old-time Democratic religion is auspicious. He has spoken eloquently of the need to redefine liberalism: the language of entitlement and rights and special-interest demands, he says, must give way to talk of responsibilities and duties."

Ever-eager for media accolades as a "moderate," President Clinton has offered little to constituents that gave him huge blocs of votes in November 1992—including African-Americans, who went 82 percent for the Clinton-Gore ticket and 89 percent for Democrats seeking House seats.

More than any other president in modern times, Clinton has pursued policies expressing contempt for large numbers of people who voted for him. But few media pundits have faulted him for that; they've been too busy urging him on.

The false assumption has been that core supporters have no choice but to vote Democratic. In fact, they *do* have another choice—to not vote at all—a choice that millions exercised on Nov. 8. As a consequence, many incumbent Democrats read the election results on pink slips.

In inner-city neighborhoods, in union halls, at a wide array of activist gatherings, a hopeful mood about Clinton's ascension to the presidency has given way to much disappointment—and anger.

This election season, a top media cliché—the mad voter—received selective treatment. The press ignored the main concerns of millions of angry Americans who didn't get much ink or air time.

They want universal health care; federal programs to create jobs; employment security, so that workers are protected from losing jobs overnight or having benefits slashed; and a reformed tax code that puts a heavier burden on the well-to-do.

But *those* angry voters are nearly invisible in the news. On election night, with returns indicating the Republican takeover of Congress, ABC anchor Peter Jennings asked "correspundit" Cokie Roberts to offer advice to Clinton. Without missing a beat, she replied: "Move to the right!"

Such advice, offered incessantly by leading voices of the

so-called "liberal media," is dubious. When the main election issues—as framed by news media and embraced by many Democrats—revolve around which party can imprison or execute the most people (or which party will slash the most taxes and government services), the Republicans have a decided advantage.

After all, if you're looking to get drunk on simplistic non-solutions, why buy "G.O.P. Lite" when you can have the real thing?

Looking ahead to 1996, speculation about President Clinton's political fortunes focuses on the match-up with the Republican presidential nominee. The assumption is that Clinton's campaign for renomination will be a cakewalk.

But if Clinton moves further rightward to appease the Republican majority in Congress, a national "Dump Clinton" campaign—coalescing around a candidate such as Jesse Jackson—might resonate with rank-and-file union members, African-Americans and other racial minorities, environmentalists, consumer activists and others.

Big media pundits and the president may be the last to notice that Clinton is not the first choice for millions of Democratic voters who see his centrist, pro-corporate proximity to Republicans as a minus, not a plus. And he could discover, too late, that "old Democrats" are part of the future as well as the past.

November 9, 1994

Part X
Scandals Hyped or Hidden

Some political dirt seems to be recycled endlessly on the front pages and the evening news. How big a "scandal" gets often depends on the political forces promoting it.

Whitewater: The Press Drowns in Story It Missed in '92

Supporters of Bill and Hillary Clinton suggest that the failed Whitewater venture from their Little Rock days is old news. The election campaign is over, the argument goes, and the voters chose Clinton.

But Whitewater never really became a campaign issue in 1992.

That's because most national media preferred to cover campaign melodrama and soundbites about "baking cookies" rather than complex stories of corporate collusion with politicians—especially when the stories weren't pushed by an establishment party or politician.

This spring [1994], leading Republicans seem to want to talk about nothing but Whitewater and the Madison Guaranty S&L. That wasn't the case during the '92 campaign.

No wonder George Bush and his allies were silent. Bush had his own—much more costly—bank scandals to worry about.

Taxpayers lost $47 million when Madison, owned by Clinton crony James McDougal, failed. But taxpayers lost $1 billion in the collapse of the Silverado S&L, which boasted "first son" Neil Bush as board member. And George Bush was implicated in the $5 billion BNL bank scandal—with BNL funds helping to arm Iraq's Saddam Hussein.

One Clinton opponent who wasn't silent about Whitewater and related issues in 1992 was Jerry Brown. Rather, he was silenced in much of the press.

As a media issue during the campaign, the whole affair rose and fell in about three weeks. Here's the history:

On March 8, 1992, investigative reporter Jeff Gerth broke the story on the front page of the *New York Times*: "Clintons Joined S&L Operator In an Ozark Real-Estate Venture." The article asserted that Bill and Hillary Clinton "were under little financial risk" in the Whitewater deal initiated by McDougal, and that Hillary and the powerful Rose law firm represented McDougal's S&L in filings before a state agency.

The next day's newspapers featured Bill Clinton's responses to the article—for example, that the venture did carry risk for the Clintons, who lost thousands.

Six days later, a *Washington Post* report scrutinized the Rose law firm's representation of various corporate clients—including Madison—in front of state regulators appointed by Gov. Clinton. "If you want something from the state," a Clinton rival was quoted, "you go to the Rose firm." The article also reported: "One of Rose's most lucrative clients is the state government."

Hours after the *Post* story broke, in a Chicago debate that was the most heated of the campaign, Jerry Brown accused Gov. Clinton of "funneling money to his wife's law firm for state business." Clinton called it a "lying accusation."

The next day, Hillary Clinton defended her husband with a feminist appeal that would be prominently quoted for days: "I suppose I could have stayed home and baked cookies and had teas. But what I decided to do was pursue my profession..."

By contrast, her revealing response to a question about whether she had represented Madison Guaranty was hardly quoted at all: "For goodness sake, you can't be a lawyer if you don't represent banks."

Although Brown's criticism was aimed at Bill—not Hillary—newspapers in the next two days were full of macho posturing from Gov. Clinton: "If somebody jumps on my wife, I'm going to jump them back." *Washington Post* columnist Richard Cohen even mocked Brown for being a bachelor: "One thing he knows nothing about—zilch, nada, zero—is marriage."

Within a week, Whitewater was virtually dead as a campaign issue. With press attention shifting to depictions of Brown as a character assassin—and discussions of "cookies" and "teas"—the issue of candidate Clinton's links to corporate power in Little Rock disappeared.

Our computer search of major dailies revealed only a few dozen articles in 1992 mentioning Whitewater or Madison—

compared to hundreds mentioning Hillary's "cookies" remark.

A key reason elite media dropped the story in 1992 was that the only newsmaker pushing it was Jerry Brown—an anti-establishment candidate who journalists were more prone to deride than quote.

These days—as if overcompensating for dropping the ball on what should have been a serious campaign issue—national media have been inflating the story.

Today's media onslaught on Whitewater is propelled day after day by quotes of outrage from Republican senators like Phil Gramm, who received favors from a Dallas operator of three failed S&Ls, and Alfonse D'Amato—whose dealings in support of friends and relatives were rebuked by the Senate Ethics Committee.

As "presidential" scandals go, this one seems distinctly gubernatorial. It's silly to compare it to Watergate, a presidential abuse of the U.S. Constitution, or Iran-Contra, which involved the White House in secret wars and arms to terrorists.

Having sidestepped the Whitewater story two years ago, many news outlets are now drowning in it.

March 30, 1994

Hypocrisy Exposes Itself in Clinton Harassment Case

In the media debate on accusations by Paula Jones against Bill Clinton, what looms large is partisan hypocrisy—while the national problem of sexual harassment has almost disappeared.

Some news outlets feel they already covered the issue during the televised Clarence Thomas/Anita Hill hearings. But, today, how well known is it that most American women experience sexual harassment? Or that 90 percent of the victims do *not* come forward—fearing retaliation or loss of privacy?

Given a green light by the Paula Jones case to pontificate about the president's genitals and alleged indecent conduct, right-wing pundits have finally found a sexual harassment claim worthy of outrage.

Although many of these conservatives have long belittled the seriousness of the workplace hazard of sexual harassment, that hasn't prevented them from becoming passionate advocates for Paula Jones.

Rush Limbaugh is one such advocate—the same Limbaugh who used to boast of the sign on his office door: "Sexual harassment at this work station will not be reported...It will be graded."

Instead of awarding Clinton an "A" for effort, Limbaugh professes indignation—and he has used the Jones case in repeated broadcasts to denounce the president.

Also indignant about Paula Jones are the sudden advocates for women's equality at the rightist *American Spectator* magazine—editor R. Emmett Tyrrell and writer David Brock. Back in 1992, Brock's error-filled "investigative" report on Anita Hill had branded her "a bit nutty and a bit slutty."

In the January [1994] issue of the *Spectator*, Brock's probe of Clinton's sex life used the claim of one Arkansas state trooper to suggest that a woman named Paula had consensual sex with the then-governor in Little Rock's Excelsior Hotel. After the encounter "which lasted no more than an hour," according to Brock, "the trooper said Paula told him she was available to be Clinton's regular girlfriend if he so desired."

If this account is true, then Jones' lawsuit is false. Or, it's just another reporting error by Brock—which hasn't slowed *Spectator* staffers from promoting Jones' harassment charge and condemning Clinton as someone who doesn't get his facts straight.

To some pundits, distinguishing between legitimate and bogus victims comes easy. Fred Barnes—who dismissed Anita Hill as "delusional"—finds Paula Jones to be "credible."

Hypocrisy also abounds among those who defend Clinton. Bellowing about the "rush to judgment...against the male" in sexual harassment cases, political talkshow host John McLaughlin rushed to judge the Jones suit as "largely bogus."

"You can sue anybody for anything," wailed McLaughlin. "There are over 100 million active lawsuits in the United States today." McLaughlin didn't mention that he himself had settled a suit for sexual harassment, after being accused by female employees.

Some Clinton defenders say the behavior alleged in the Jones suit is simply too crude to be believed (though Clinton's claim that he never met her seems more dubious). Other defenders suggest that—*even as alleged*—the behavior is too trivial to be making such a big deal over. This latter argument amounts to an apology for sexual abuse by powerful men.

Discussing the lawsuit on CBS's *Face the Nation*, Joe Klein of *Newsweek* carried on about his fears that "no one with any interesting aspects of their past" will run for office. "We're going to wind up with government by goody-goodies," he lamented. Klein then propounded his absurd theory that "having an interesting sexual history is a leading indicator of success in the presidency."

Asked about the Jones lawsuit on NBC's *Meet the Press*, liberal columnist Mary McGrory offered her view that "this debate was held two years ago in New Hampshire, where people knew that this president was not a model husband."

But voters elected someone who had tacitly acknowledged extramarital activities—consensual ones—*not* unwelcome sexual advances toward an employee whose future he could influence.

The failure to distinguish between consensual and non-consensual behavior is not uncommon in media discourse that finds little room for knowledgeable, independent experts on sexual harassment.

Amid the blizzard of partisan cross-talk in the media, all that's clear is the hypocrisy—whether from the conservatives who momentarily champion working women against harassment, or the Clinton apologists who make light of a grave workplace issue.

May 11, 1994

Newt in the News:
Will Journalists Be Intimidated?

As the faces of power shift in Washington, so do relations between politicians and the news media.

No relationship will be more fascinating to watch than that of incoming House speaker Newt Gingrich and the national press corps.

Will mainstream media scrutinize Gingrich as they have Bill Clinton—comparing his words and deeds, bringing up old scandals and contradictions, probing his personal life and finances? If so, Mr. Gingrich may be in deep trouble.

Or will news outlets—afraid that Gingrich might accuse them of "liberal bias" or question their patriotism—retreat in fear?

A master of intimidation and attack, Gingrich is one of a few politicians we can compare to Sen. Joe McCarthy without being hyperbolic.

Although he's already complaining about unfair media treatment in the wake of the Republican triumph, there was only sporadic critical coverage of Gingrich *before* Election Day—much of it sparked by his ugly attacks near the close of the campaign.

Days before the election, in an unsavory exploitation of tragedy in South Carolina, Gingrich imputed blame for Susan Smith's infanticide to Democratic Party rule. "The only way you can get change," Gingrich said in reference to the killings, "is to vote Republican." As it happens, Smith's step-father (who played a big role in raising her) is a Republican and local leader of the Christian Coalition; imagine how Gingrich would have howled if Democrats had played politics with that fact.

But wild charges have long been Gingrich's stock in trade. In 1984, he accused Democrats of being "blind to communism"; he threatened to "file charges" against ten members of Congress over their stance on Nicaragua. He accused a congressman of disseminating "communist propaganda" on Capitol Hill.

It was Gingrich who labeled Kitty Dukakis a "drug addict." His GOPAC political action committee once put out a mailing that advised Republican candidates to "talk like Newt" by calling Democrats "traitors." He has called Democrats the "enemy of normal people" and the party of "total weirdness." Someone in his office helped circulate rumors that House speaker Tom Foley was gay.

A walking web of contradictions, Gingrich's talk and actions cry out for tough media scrutiny. He's a nine-term congressman campaigning for term limits; a critic of most recent military interventions who still demands budget hikes for the Pentagon; a Vietnam-aged hawk who didn't fight in the war, but scorns Clinton for not being "militarily competent."

Though he's long crusaded against "the liberal welfare state" and opposes "sending more money to inner-city mayors," he's no foe of federal aid to well-to-do suburbia. His district is in Cobb County, Georgia, an affluent area that receives more federal money than all but two suburbs in America.

As *Common Cause* magazine documented in 1993, his suburban constituents are "hooked on federal handouts"—for schools, roads, police, airport, military contracts, economic development, etc. Gingrich refused to discuss *welfare for the well-off* with *Common Cause*, but journalists should pursue this contradiction.

Another story worth pursuing is Gingrich's "Renewing American Civilization" course, transmitted via satellite to colleges thanks to lavish funding from corporate supporters, who gain a tax deduction. The course, which explicitly excludes liberal ideas, helps recruit Republican activists.

The introductory essay by Gingrich extols "entrepreneurial free enterprise" and the McDonald's fast-food chain. Gingrich's course is not "PC" (politically correct). It's "CC"—corporately correct.

Ironically, Gingrich gained renown for dethroning former House speaker Jim Wright by sparking an ethics probe into the finances behind Wright's autobiography. If the House Ethics Committee—now probing Gingrich and GOPAC's financial role in this supposedly nonpartisan, educational course—fumbles after Republicans take over the House, will journalists pick up the ball?

And will they expose the fact that Gingrich, an apostle of lean and clean government, has made a career of obstructing campaign and lobbying reform? His GOPAC doesn't even identify its donors.

While most mainstream journalists shy away from a politician's personal life, Gingrich's finger-pointing antics invite examination—on grounds of extreme hypocrisy. Take the issue of "family values." His entry into Congress in 1978 was facilitated by attacks on his Democratic opponent for her plans to commute between Washington and Georgia, where her family would remain. "Newt's family is like your family," said a flyer. An ad declared: "When elected, Newt will keep his family together."

But 18 months later, Gingrich's family came apart when he left his wife. She says that Gingrich demanded that she sign a divorce paper in her hospital bed, where she lay recovering from cancer surgery.

While Gingrich campaigned for "a return to moral values," he sought out extramarital affairs, reported *Mother Jones* magazine in an October 1984 profile.

Asked by the *Mother Jones* reporter if he was having an affair in 1980 with his second wife before filing for divorce from his first, Gingrich did not deny it. Yet there he was in 1983, demanding that two congressmen be expelled from the House for their sexual affairs. "A free country," intoned Gingrich, "must have honest leaders if it is to remain free."

Ever since his Nov. 8 election triumph, Gingrich has pontificated about moral and family decline. Yet his ex-wife had to go to court to get adequate child support from him, and the pastor at Gingrich's church had to take up a collection for the congressman's family. In 1993, his former wife went to court again, alleging that Gingrich had not kept up with alimony and other payments.

On the Gingrich watch, journalists will have their hands full—if they don't duck and run for cover.

November 16, 1994

Part XI
Hidden History

As the saying goes: **Those who control the present control the past; those who control the past control the future.** *Media renditions of history are so selective that key facts and events are liable to be buried.*

Do the Founding Fathers
Benefit From Media Bias?

Patriotic holidays come and go, but one theme remains fairly constant in our country's mass media: The Founding Fathers were a sterling bunch of guys.

Their press notices were the usual raves this July Fourth—superficial accolades for leaders of the struggle for independence.

"The Founding Fathers," according to the New York daily *Newsday*, "declared that they were willing to fight for the principles of freedom and self-determination, and then went on to create a form of government that has allowed its people to endure and prosper."

The *Orlando Sentinel* issued a typical proclamation: "The Fourth of July, the birthday of this grand experiment in human liberty, should be a reminder of what it's all about—not material wealth or political advantages, but human freedom. Those who made the American Revolution are its best explainers."

While such puffery was making its accustomed rounds this Fourth of July, other perspectives occasionally reached newsprint. "From the outset, ordinary people decried America's great contradiction—proclaiming liberty for all while practicing slavery," wrote Linda R. Monk in the St. Louis *Post-Dispatch*. Columnist Vernon Jarrett of the *Chicago Sun-Times* was blunt: "Among the Founding Fathers, there was no broad commitment to freedom for all."

It's true that the famed men of the American Revolution were brave, eloquent and visionary as they challenged the British despot, King George III. But present-day news media usually avoid acknowledging an uncomfortable fact: Many heroes of American independence didn't seem to mind very much when *they* benefitted from injustice.

Take the brilliant man who wrote the Declaration of Independence, 218 years ago. Thomas Jefferson certainly had a passion for freedom: "We hold these truths to be self-evident, that all men are created equal, that they are endowed by their Creator with certain unalienable Rights…"

All men? Not quite. The luxuries of Monticello were made possible by slavery. Jefferson may have wrestled with his conscience, but it lost. He remained a slave-owner until he died.

As for women, forget it. Jefferson assumed that females should have no right to own property, or to vote. Women, he contended, would be "too wise to wrinkle their foreheads with politics."

The truth be told, some of the leading patriots were downright greedy.

George Washington was America's richest man. And he had a record as a land speculator that makes Donald Trump seem like a penny-ante realtor. After the Revolutionary War, Washington used his enormous wealth and power to snap up vast tracts of land.

Patrick Henry was also among the heroic fighters for independence who went on to make a killing in westward real estate. After demanding "Give me liberty or give me death," Henry wanted Indians out of the way. His slogan could have become: "Give me property or give them death."

James Madison and many other founders of the United States were masters of large plantations. They made sure that the U.S. Constitution would perpetuate slavery: counting each slave as three-fifths of a person, with no rights.

Is this just old, irrelevant history—dredged up from water over the dam? Not at all.

Turning a blind eye to ugly aspects of the past can be a bad habit that carries over into the present: Too often, journalists and media commentators focus on P.R. facades (old or new), and pay little attention to the people left out of the pretty picture.

In *A People's History of the United States,* author Howard Zinn observes: "The point of noting those outside the arc of human rights in the Declaration [of Independence] is not…to lay impossible moral burdens on that time. It is to try to understand the way in which the Declaration functioned to mobilize certain groups of Americans, ignoring others."

Back in 1776, all the flowery oratory about freedom did nothing for black slaves, women, indentured servants or Native Americans. If we forget that fact, we are remembering only fairy tales instead of history.

During the Constitution's 1987 bicentennial, Supreme Court Justice Thurgood Marshall punctured the time-honored idolatry of the Constitution's framers: "The government they devised was defective from the start, requiring several amendments, a civil war and momentous social transformation to attain the...respect for individual freedoms and human rights we hold as fundamental today."

Most of the delegates who gathered in Philadelphia to draw up the Constitution were wealthy. And they "were determined that persons of birth and fortune should control the affairs of the nation and check the 'leveling impulses' of the propertyless multitude that composed 'the majority faction,'" writes political scientist Michael Parenti.

In his book *Democracy for the Few*, Parenti notes: "The delegates spent many weeks debating their interests, but these were the differences of merchants, slave owners, and manufacturers, a debate of haves versus haves in which each group sought safeguards within the new Constitution for its particular concerns."

However, "there were no dirt farmers or poor artisans attending the convention to proffer an opposing viewpoint. The debate between haves and have-nots never occurred." And "the delegates repeatedly stated their intention to erect a government strong enough to protect the haves from the have-nots."

After two centuries, you'd hope that more journalists would be willing to set aside fawning myths about the Founding Fathers. If that happens, the emergence of candor might even help to shed some light on the Ruling Fathers of today.

July 6, 1994

Glimmers of History Improve Coverage of Native Americans

Time will tell whether it's a journalistic trend or merely a fad. But Cable News Network may have started something in recent weeks with its 20-part series, "Native Americans: The Invisible People."

During November [1994], CNN viewers saw numerous well-researched reports venturing beyond the usual media treatment of Indians to explore what rarely gets much air time—in a word, *history*.

Most news outlets are loath to recount the realities—recurring betrayals, broken treaties and virtual genocide—inflicted on this continent's native peoples over the course of 500 years.

The customary media approach is akin to assessing what's on stage without considering the play's earlier acts. Typical news items are brief snapshots of current conditions—high rates of unemployment and alcoholism on Indian reservations, or disputes that involve fishing rights or gambling casinos—without historical context.

Television tends to be the worst media offender. But CNN broke away from the pattern with "The Invisible People." What distinguished the network's special reports was attention to the content of treaties.

"When a government makes an agreement with another nation, that government is expected to abide by the terms of the agreement," said a CNN anchor, introducing one segment. "But many Native American nations are struggling to uphold rights granted in treaties with the United States."

Correspondent Stephen Frazier explained that more than 150 years ago, a pact with the Mille Lacs band of Ojibwa Indians "reserved the right to gather and hunt and fish on the land they were giving up. Otherwise, they said, they would starve." Although the U.S. government signed the treaty, "when Minnesota became a state it deliberately did not recognize any treaty privileges of Indians."

The CNN story gave coverage to foes of Indian rights, like the Minneapolis businessman who blasted Indian activism as "political revisionism of history." But the report also provided a platform for defenders of Indian treaty rights.

The Mille Lacs won their court case last summer. And, correspondent Frazier concluded, "157 years after the Mille Lacs made a treaty with the United States, it is still valid. It is still the law of the land. It must still be respected."

Without historical explanation, the Mille Lacs' court victory—retaining special hunting and fishing rights—might have seemed unfair to viewers. With the factual background, it was much more likely to seem just.

In another CNN segment, focusing on a land dispute in Nevada, correspondent Bonnie Anderson explained that "the only treaty between the United States and the Western Shoshone was signed here in Ruby Valley in 1863 and it seemed to affirm the Indians' ownership of the land." In modern times, most Western Shoshone people "did not want money for land they did not want to sell."

Reporting from Indiana, CNN chronicled the struggle of Miami Indians to regain tribal recognition from the U.S. government. Across the country, "150 tribes have petitioned the Bureau of Indian Affairs but the odds are against them. Thus far fewer than a dozen have been recognized."

And, near the Grand Canyon, CNN spotlighted an example of how lucrative projects—in this case uranium mining—can run roughshod over Indian spiritual rights. A woman who is part of the Havasupai tribe said, "It's sacrilegious to go build a mine or make a profit off of an area which people respect and consider sacred or is part of their culture or their religion."

As CNN's Anderson reported: "Tribes across the United States are waging similar battles to protect more than 50 sites sacred to them. But they're up against formidable opponents, like oil, gas and logging companies—modern-day enemies armed with big bucks and industry-friendly laws. So far, Native

Americans have not won a single sacred sites dispute based on the First Amendment's guarantee of freedom of religion."

In a poignant moment, a Native American activist commented: "I don't believe that if these were Christian sites important to mainline religions that we would see them being bulldozed without any legal protection."

The executive director of the Native American Journalists Association, Ruth Denny, told us that she had "mixed feelings" about the CNN series. She noted that the network's founder, Ted Turner, has helped to perpetuate negative stereotypes with his Atlanta Braves baseball team and its "tomahawk chop."

In the future, you may be seeing a lot more Native Americans on network television. CBS has announced plans for a major eight-hour series about North American Indians, to be hosted and co-produced by Kevin Costner.

Whether such upcoming TV projects will represent genuine progress, or just a Hollywood gloss, remains to be seen.

November 23, 1994

Author of *The Jungle*
Was a Fierce Media Critic

This year [1993] many news stories about tainted beef have credited Upton Sinclair's novel *The Jungle* with forcing the federal government to establish a meat-inspection program back in 1907.

It's true that the novel—with its nauseating depiction of Chicago meat-packing plants—quickly led the U.S. Department of Agriculture to begin inspections. But recent press accounts haven't mentioned key aspects of the author's battles with "the Beef Trust."

If he were alive today, Upton Sinclair probably would not be surprised that E. coli bacteria had harmed hundreds of people 87 years after his novel caused such a stir. As Sinclair saw it, the 1907 law never amounted to much: "The lobbyists of the packers had their way in Washington; the meat inspection bill was deprived of all its sharpest teeth, and in that form [President Theodore] Roosevelt accepted it..."

Most of all, Sinclair blamed the news media. "Because of the kindness of American editorial writers to the interests which contribute full-page advertisements to newspapers," he wrote a dozen years after the law went into effect, "the American people still have their meat prepared in filth."

In those days, of course, print media were the *only* news media. From the outset, the press gave *The Jungle* a rough reception. "Can it be possible that any one is deceived by this insane rant and drivel?" one widely syndicated newspaper column scoffed. The meat industry mailed out a million copies of that article.

"I was determined to get something done about the atrocious conditions under which men, women and children were working in the Chicago stockyards," Sinclair recalled. "In my efforts to get something done, I was like an animal in a cage. The bars of this cage were newspapers, which stood between me and the public; and inside the cage I roamed up and down, testing one bar after another, and finding them impossible to break."

Sinclair developed intense enmity toward the Associated Press (and vice versa). "Throughout my entire campaign against the Beef Trust," he wrote in 1919, AP's editors "never sent out a single line injurious to the interests of the packers, save for a few lines dealing with the Congressional hearings, which they could not entirely suppress."

Upton Sinclair came to see the problem as chronic. "American newspapers as a whole represent private interests and not public interests," he declared. "But there will be occasions upon which exception to this rule is made; for in order to be of any use at all, the newspapers must have a circulation, and to get circulation they must pretend to care about the public." To Sinclair it was all too apparent that "American Journalism is a class institution, serving the rich and spurning the poor."

In May 1914, labor strife drew Sinclair to Colorado in the wake of the "Ludlow Massacre." Armed thugs working for the Rockefeller mining interests had killed women and children in a tent colony of striking coal miners and their families. Sinclair seethed at what he called a "concrete wall" that kept accurate information from the American people.

It was the mighty AP wire service that infuriated Sinclair most of all. "The directors and managers of the Associated Press were as directly responsible for the subsequent starvation of these thousands of Colorado mine-slaves as if they had taken them and strangled them with their naked fingers," he contended.

Sinclair presented AP with evidence that Colorado's governor had lied to President Woodrow Wilson about the state's role in the miners' strike. When the news agency refused to report on the matter, Sinclair rushed to the Denver telegraph office and cabled the information himself to 20 of the nation's biggest newspapers.

He later observed: "There was no capitalist magazine or newspaper in the United States that would take up the conduct of the Associated Press in the Colorado strike."

Sinclair expounded on his media critique in a nonfiction book titled *The Brass Check*, which he published himself in 1920. It went through six printings and 100,000 copies within a half-year—though the book is difficult to locate today.

"I do not expect to please contemporary Journalism," he wrote, "but I expect to produce a book which the student of the future will recognize as just." As far as Sinclair was concerned, "Journalism is one of the devices whereby industrial autocracy keeps its control over political democracy."

Such an attitude, expressed by a tireless and renowned author year after year, did not exactly endear Upton Sinclair to newspaper executives around the country.

When Sinclair moved to Southern California and gave a speech to the Friday Morning Club of Los Angeles, an editorial in the *Los Angeles Times*—headlined "UPTON SINCLAIR'S RAVINGS"—lamented that "the club rostrum should be used for such ungodly purposes" by "an effeminate young man with a fatuous smile, a weak chin and a sloping forehead, talking in a false treble" and uttering "weak, pernicious, vile doctrines." Soon after World War I ended, the *L.A. Times* spearheaded a campaign to jail Sinclair as a subversive.

In 1934—after more than a quarter-century of doing battle with the major news outlets in the country—Upton Sinclair almost became governor of California. Running on a campaign platform called "End Poverty In California"(EPIC), Sinclair won the state's Democratic primary.

State business leaders panicked. They took the unprecedented step of hiring an ad agency to warn that election of the Socialist-turned-Democrat would destroy California. In another innovation, Hollywood studios saw to it that newsreels smearing Sinclair would fill movie theaters throughout the state.

Despite the intense media battering that included constant denunciations by the *Los Angeles Times, San Francisco Chronicle* and other powerful daily papers, Sinclair was able to win 38 percent of the votes in a three-person race.

Today Upton Sinclair is known mainly for *The Jungle*. But he should also be remembered as a courageous media critic and activist who took his lumps from the press lords for speaking his mind and his heart.

May 19, 1993

30-Year Anniversary: Tonkin Gulf Lie Launched Vietnam War

Thirty years ago, it all seemed very clear.

"AMERICAN PLANES HIT NORTH VIETNAM AFTER SECOND ATTACK ON OUR DESTROYERS; MOVE TAKEN TO HALT NEW AGGRESSION," announced a *Washington Post* headline on Aug. 5, 1964.

That same day, the front page of the *New York Times* reported: "President Johnson has ordered retaliatory action against gunboats and 'certain supporting facilities in North Vietnam' after renewed attacks against American destroyers in the Gulf of Tonkin."

But there was no "second attack" by North Vietnam—no "renewed attacks against American destroyers." By reporting official claims as absolute truths, American journalism opened the floodgates for the bloody Vietnam War.

And a pattern took hold: continuous government lies passed on by pliant mass media...leading to over 55,000 American deaths and millions of Vietnamese casualties.

The official story was that North Vietnamese torpedo boats launched an "unprovoked attack" against a U.S. destroyer on "routine patrol" in the Tonkin Gulf on Aug. 2—and that North Vietnamese PT boats followed up with a "deliberate attack" on a pair of U.S. ships two days later.

The truth was very different.

Rather than being on a routine patrol Aug. 2, the U.S. destroyer *Maddox* was actually engaged in aggressive intelligence-gathering maneuvers—in sync with coordinated attacks on North Vietnam by the South Vietnamese navy and the Laotian air force.

"The day before, two attacks on North Vietnam...had taken place," writes scholar Daniel C. Hallin. Those assaults were "part of a campaign of increasing military pressure on the

North that the United States had been pursuing since early 1964."

On the night of Aug. 4, the Pentagon proclaimed that a second attack by North Vietnamese PT boats had occurred earlier that day in the Tonkin Gulf—a report cited by President Johnson as he went on national TV that evening to announce a momentous escalation in the war: air strikes against North Vietnam.

But Johnson ordered U.S. bombers to "retaliate" for a North Vietnamese torpedo attack that never happened.

Prior to the U.S. air strikes, top officials in Washington had reason to doubt that any Aug. 4 attack by North Vietnam had occurred. Cables from the U.S. task force commander in the Tonkin Gulf, Captain John J. Herrick, referred to "freak weather effects," "almost total darkness" and an "overeager sonarman" who "was hearing ship's own propeller beat."

One of the U.S. Navy pilots flying overhead that night was squadron commander James Stockdale, who gained fame later as a POW and then Ross Perot's vice presidential candidate. "I had the best seat in the house to watch that event," recalled Stockdale a few years ago, "and our destroyers were just shooting at phantom targets—there were no PT boats there.... There was nothing there but black water and American fire power."

In 1965, Lyndon Johnson commented: "For all I know, our Navy was shooting at whales out there."

But Johnson's deceitful speech of Aug. 4, 1964, won accolades from editorial writers. The president, proclaimed the *New York Times*, "went to the American people last night with the somber facts." The *Los Angeles Times* urged Americans to "face the fact that the Communists, by their attack on American vessels in international waters, have themselves escalated the hostilities."

An exhaustive new book, *The War Within: America's Battle Over Vietnam*, begins with a dramatic account of the Tonkin Gulf incidents. In an interview, author Tom Wells told us that American media "described the air strikes that Johnson launched in response as merely 'tit for tat'—when in reality they reflected plans the administration had already drawn up for gradually increasing its overt military pressure against the North."

Why such inaccurate news coverage? Wells points to the media's "almost exclusive reliance on U.S. government officials as sources of information"—as well as "reluctance to question official pronouncements on 'national security issues.'"

Daniel Hallin's classic book *The "Uncensored War"* observes that journalists had "a great deal of information available which contradicted the official account [of Tonkin Gulf events]; it simply wasn't used. The day before the first incident, Hanoi had protested the attacks on its territory by Laotian aircraft and South Vietnamese gunboats."

What's more, "It was generally known...that 'covert' operations against North Vietnam, carried out by South Vietnamese forces with U.S. support and direction, had been going on for some time."

In the absence of independent journalism, the Gulf of Tonkin Resolution—the closest thing there ever was to a declaration of war against North Vietnam—sailed through Congress on Aug. 7. (Two courageous senators, Wayne Morse of Oregon and Ernest Gruening of Alaska, provided the only "no" votes.) The resolution authorized the president "to take all necessary measures to repel any armed attack against the forces of the United States and to prevent further aggression."

The rest is tragic history.

July 27, 1994

Press Tributes to Nixon
Dishonor the Dead

Don't speak ill of the dead.

It's an accepted custom—one that's been shaping media reminiscences of Richard Nixon.

But the rule against speaking unkindly of the deceased is no license to distort history. That dishonors other dead—including those who lost their lives because of Nixon's policies.

The conventional wisdom in the press is that Watergate tarnished a presidency characterized by foreign policy triumphs. According to many obituaries, Watergate resulted from a character flaw of paranoia; but in foreign affairs, Nixon was clear-thinking and far-sighted.

To make the case for Nixon as foreign policy master, unwanted historical facts have to be shuffled, shrunk or ignored.

Virtually every media retrospective hails Nixon for opening U.S. relations with China in 1972. Yet—if it was "genius" to begin dialogue with the state that governed almost one-fourth of the human race—what brand of folly was it to have spent most of the previous 20 years demonizing other Americans who proposed just such a common-sense move?

Nixon had been a charter member of the "China Lobby," which reacted to the Maoist revolution by initiating purges in Washington against diplomats who had "lost China"—ruining the careers of thoughtful Americans. Policy debate on China was stifled for nearly two decades. What was the ingenious solution foisted on our country by this lobby? Pretending that the island of Taiwan—home of exiled Gen. Chiang Kai-shek—was the real China.

Vietnam was another of Nixon's "foreign-policy accomplishments of historic proportions," in the words of the *New York Times:* "After at first broadening and intensifying the conflict in Indochina, he ended U.S. involvement in the fighting there."

This summary of Nixon's role in Vietnam ignores the fact that he campaigned in 1968 as something of a peace candidate, claiming to have a "secret plan" to end the war. What was the "plan"? Escalation.

Nixon didn't end "U.S. involvement in the fighting." He prolonged it. Over 25,000 U.S. soldiers and a half-million Vietnamese—most of them civilians—were killed as President Nixon pursued the war, despite opposition from increasing numbers of Americans.

U.S. military advisers were still backing a corrupt South Vietnamese government until it fell in April 1975—eight months after Nixon resigned. He hardly deserves praise for "ending" the war, or U.S. involvement in it.

One country neglected in news accounts praising Nixon is Cambodia. A focus on his Cambodia policy—which was illegal and deadly—would undermine portrayals of Nixon as a foreign policy whiz.

In March 1969, two months after taking office, Nixon ordered the secret bombing of Cambodia in pursuit of Vietnamese communist bases. In the next 14 months, the U.S. flew 3,630 bombing raids over Cambodia—whose neutrality in the Cold War and the Vietnam War infuriated Washington. Military records were falsified to hide the bombing from Congress.

In March 1970, Cambodia's neutralist Prince Norodom Sihanouk was neatly ousted in a military coup smiled on by the Nixon administration. The next month, the U.S. widened the Indochina War by invading Cambodia—causing massive numbers of civilian casualties and refugees.

The Nixon intervention plunged a once peaceful, neutral Cambodia into chaos, war and dislocation that led inexorably to the victory of the murderous Khmer Rouge in 1975. On the eve of their seizure of power, Republican Congressman Pete McCloskey declared that what the U.S. had done to Cambodia was a "greater evil than we have done to any country in the world."

In recent days, almost every media review of Nixon's life

has politely ignored a five-letter word: Chile. Although an obsession for his administration, that country is not cited as one of Nixon's "foreign-policy achievements."

Nixon and top adviser Henry Kissinger did *achieve* their objective in Chile, which was to prevent the elected president—democratic socialist Salvador Allende—from serving his six-year term. They ended up destroying one of Latin America's oldest parliamentary democracies, replacing it with a brutal military dictatorship that ruled for 16 years.

While media reports have noted that Watergate brought words like "cover-up" and "stonewalling" into the lexicon, they didn't mention that Nixon's effort to subvert Chilean democracy introduced another word into the language: "destabilization."

As documented in U.S. Senate reports, Nixon administration operatives and the CIA undermined the Chilean economy, sabotaging loans and fomenting strikes. They bribed journalists in Chile to lie about Allende and incite chaos. They plotted the murder of the Chilean Army's commander because he was loyal to democracy. And they repeatedly pushed the military to stage a coup.

After three years of such destabilization, a military junta struck, dropping bombs on the presidential palace. Allende died inside. Thousands of Chilean democrats were executed.

Pardon us if we seem to be violating the rule against speaking ill of a recently deceased U.S. president. But we keep thinking of that other president, Salvador Allende, who didn't live to see the age of 81.

Richard Nixon's foreign policies were often deadly. When news reports obscure that reality, terms like "cover-up" and "stonewalling" are quite apt.

April 27, 1994

TOM TOMORROW ©11-23-93

Part XII
Human Rights Abroad

Some human rights stories are vividly rendered, in horrifying detail; others go untold or glossed over. In a world where atrocities are widespread, why does the U.S. media spotlight fall only on certain horrors? And how do news outlets designate their villains and heroes?

Human Rights and Media Wrongs

Last month in Vienna, the United Nations brought together representatives from 170 countries for a World Conference on Human Rights.

The [June 1993] conference discussed some subjects, like Bosnia, that are front-page news here, and other issues that Americans hear far less about—such as atrocities in Angola committed by Jonas Savimbi's guerrillas, formerly armed by the U.S. government.

Selective news coverage of global human rights abuses has a long journalistic history in the United States. It's a practice that has deadly effects.

When a U.S.-backed government violating human rights receives tough, persistent coverage in American news outlets, it can change Washington's policy toward that government. Lives can be saved.

But many regimes are able to engage in torture, murder and mass jailings with almost no U.S. media coverage.

Over the years, various studies have analyzed why certain tyrants get front-page attention, but others can commit abuses in relative privacy. A big factor is that U.S. media outlets usually don't set their own foreign news agenda; they let the White House lead. And American administrations are anything but "objective"—their P.R. goal is to highlight brutal enemies, while turning the spotlight away from brutal friends.

Take the case of Saddam Hussein. Prior to Iraq's 1990 invasion of Kuwait, when Hussein was a U.S. ally, the dictator's crimes were well-documented—but hardly mentioned in American media. In 1985, for example, Amnesty International issued a report detailing Iraq's torture of hundreds of children to extract information about their relatives. It met with a giant yawn in the U.S. media.

Certainly the White House—busy offering Iraq credits, intelligence support and arms in the mid-1980s—had no interest in shining a light on Hussein's abuses then.

But after the Kuwait invasion, journalists outdid even President Bush in depicting Hussein as a "beast" and a "monster." When Hussein posed for pictures with a young British hostage, the New York *Post* front page carried the huge headline: "CHILD ABUSER."

Years earlier, when Washington's support was helping Hussein torture Iraqi children and adults, such journalistic outrage could have made a difference.

Or take the case of China's Deng Xiaoping. U.S. media coverage of the Tiananmen Square uprising and crackdown in 1989 was infused with righteous indignation. But what about media coverage in the mid-1980s—when thousands of students and dissidents were being tortured, while millions of Chinese languished in labor camps and prisons? This was a period when President Reagan approved sales of police equipment to Deng's internal security forces, and expanded military ties with China.

Much of the coverage hailed the "enlightened" Deng as a "liberalizer" and "reformer" who supported "free enterprise." *Time* magazine cheered Deng Xiaoping, selecting him "Man of the Year" for 1985.

After the Tiananmen crackdown, *New York Times* columnist A.M. Rosenthal complained that "American administrations yawned at reports of repression of basic freedoms in China.... So, much too often, did American journalism."

Rosenthal was an odd one to complain, since he'd been the executive editor of the *New York Times* during the mid-1980s when its coverage of repression in China virtually ceased. From 1984 through 1986, *Newsweek* featured only one report on the subject; *Time* published none.

Given these historical examples, news consumers have reason to wonder what major human rights dramas may be unfolding today outside the frame of most mainstream media.

Is it the struggle to end the nearly three-decade-long Mobutu dictatorship in Zaire, a regime long supported by the U.S. government?

Is it the effort to win an accounting of 1,600 Greek Cypriots missing since Northern Cyprus was occupied by Turkey, another U.S. ally?

Or perhaps it's the challenge to a brutal military in Guatemala which has effectively held power since a U.S.-backed invasion and coup in 1954?

If you're a viewer of *Rights & Wrongs*—the national TV show devoted to global human rights—you know about these issues.

Don't blame yourself if you've never seen *Rights & Wrongs*. Blame PBS, which has refused to fund or distribute the program.

PBS seems wary of a weekly series willing to point out Washington's complicity in human rights abuses. The program's producers—Globalvision in New York—have had to self-distribute the show to individual public TV stations. At many stations, it airs at off hours.

If PBS executives find the backbone to support the show, which is hosted by Charlayne Hunter-Gault, the program's survival will be assured.

In that case, you'll be able to tune in to *Rights & Wrongs* for the full story the next time the White House sends aid to a tyrant who tortures kids, or when *Time* magazine salutes a leading human rights abuser as its "Man of the Year."

July 7, 1993

20 Years After Chile Coup—Media Coverage Still Evasive

Twenty years ago the bloody hands of dictatorship strangled democracy in Chile.

On Sept. 11, 1973, a military junta struck—bombing the presidential palace in Santiago, rounding up political activists, and seizing the media. When the smoke cleared, the country's elected president, Salvador Allende, was dead.

Thousands were executed, tens of thousands jailed. Chile became a land of torture and repression under General Augusto Pinochet. But U.S. news media shed little light on what caused the coup, and what happened in its wake.

Many reporters took their cues from the Nixon White House, which had special venom for Allende—a Marxist elected to a six-year term as Chile's president.

Back in 1964, the U.S. had poured $20 million into Chile to help defeat Allende's first campaign for the presidency. When Allende won the popular vote in 1970, top U.S. officials were furious.

They tried—unsuccessfully—to prevent Salvador Allende from taking office. Among the many gambits: The CIA paid 23 journalists from ten countries to rush to Chile and write dire articles about the consequences if Allende became president; the reports sparked a huge bank panic in Santiago, leading to the transfer of large amounts of capital overseas.

Allende's "Popular Unity" campaign had pledged to fight poverty by providing nutrition, health care, education and employment to millions of impoverished Chileans. During the early 1970s, Chile's new government set about making good on its promises.

But corporations with big investments in Chile were eager to see an end to the socialist government. ITT pushed U.S. policymakers to move against Allende. So did Pepsico—whose board chairman and CEO, Donald M. Kendall, was close friends with President Nixon.

191

Kendall beseeched Nixon and his foreign policy chief Henry Kissinger to intensify covert operations. The White House moved to fulfill a plan approved in a meeting that involved CIA Director Richard Helms, Nixon and Kissinger: "Make the [Chilean] economy scream," Helms wrote in his notes.

In a cable sent to Washington when Allende was about to take office, U.S. Ambassador Edward M. Korrey reported telling Chilean authorities: "Not a nut or bolt will be allowed to reach Chile under Allende. Once Allende comes to power we shall do all within our power to condemn Chile and Chileans to utmost deprivation and poverty, a policy designed for a long time to come."

Washington followed through on its threats. And, as the economic squeeze took its toll, U.S. agencies also stepped up the media war inside Chile. The CIA funneled money and a massive flow of anti-Allende propaganda into the Chilean newspaper *El Mercurio*, which played a crucial role in fomenting turmoil and setting the stage for the coup in 1973.

At about 9:20 a.m. on Sept. 11, with bombs exploding nearby, Salvador Allende spoke from the presidential palace on a radio station not yet blown off the air: "Having a historic choice to make, I shall sacrifice my life to be loyal to my people and I can assure you that I am certain that the seeds planted by us in the noble consciences of thousands and thousands of Chileans will never be prevented from growing."

In the United States, congressional inquiries during the mid-1970s illuminated deep CIA involvement in the overthrow of Chile's elected government. But, while the torture and repression continued, media attention on Chile was low in quantity and quality.

In 1984, a typical article in the *New York Times* recounted that Allende's policies caused "chaos" which "brought in the military"—conveniently omitting mention of the pivotal roles played by the CIA, other U.S. agencies and corporations eager to protect their holdings inside Chile.

In August 1988 the *New York Times* front page ran a photo

of a grandfatherly-looking Pinochet—over the heading "Pinochet to Seek a Third Term." The caption explained that he was "nominated to run in the Oct. 5 single-candidate election."

In fact, Gen. Pinochet was holding a plebiscite designed to perpetuate his reign. He wasn't running for any kind of third term. He'd never been elected to any office. Nor was he "nominated" by anyone other than a clique of military officers.

Pinochet lost much of his power in 1989—but U.S. news coverage has continued the old evasions. "The media make you believe that living under the junta wasn't that bad," observes Chilean exile Claudio Duran, now a Californian.

Although the dictatorship savagely attacked the poor, you wouldn't know that from U.S. media crowing about Chile's economic "boom" over the last decade.

The economy has been "anything but miraculous" for Chile's working people, writes Cornell University scholar Cathy Schneider in the magazine *Report on the Americas*. Forty-two percent of Chileans were living in poverty by the end of the 1980s. "Poverty and income inequality which grew by colossal proportions during the years of the Pinochet dictatorship have scarcely been addressed by the new democratic regime."

Today, Schneider writes, "the Chilean government provides funds only to those popular organizations willing to convert into small businesses. Many soup kitchens, for example, have become private bakeries, groceries or restaurants with government support. The entrepreneur is encouraged, the political organizer is repressed."

Seeing the world through the eyes of the wealthy, the *New York Times* recently reported: "Economists and bankers generally agree" that Chile ranks second among "the most attractive Latin American countries for investment." The article lauded Chile as Latin America's "fastest-growing and perhaps most open economy."

The newspaper added: "Chile is a good example of heightened investment by consumer-product and technology companies. Pepsico late last year announced a $100 million investment program, buying the country's largest bottler and snack-food concerns, and opening KFC's and Pizza Huts in Santiago."

There's another side—a bloody one—to the Pepsico story in Chile. But you probably won't find it anywhere in news media coverage of Chile. Maybe the place you're least likely to hear about Pepsico's role in the murder of Chilean democracy is the *MacNeil/Lehrer NewsHour*, sponsored by Pepsico to the tune of several million dollars every year.

September 8, 1993

Haiti News Coverage
Leaves Out Vital History

These days [autumn 1993] Americans are seeing a lot of news coverage about Haiti. But instead of candid history, we've been getting journalistic myths. Plenty of them.

THE U.S. GOVERNMENT AS INNOCENT DO-GOODER

"Washington has a long and troubled history with Port-au-Prince," *Newsweek* reported in its Oct. 25 [1993] issue. The magazine recalled the 19-year occupation of Haiti by U.S. Marines that ended in 1934—but, like other news outlets, skimmed over more recent history.

While informing readers that Francois ("Papa Doc") Duvalier and his son Jean-Claude ("Baby Doc") went on to "tyrannize Haiti for 30 years," *Newsweek* didn't get around to mentioning the U.S. government's support for their bloodthirsty dictatorship.

Nor did *Newsweek* mention that the Reagan administration was hailing the dictatorship as late as 1985—when a *Washington Post* headline read: "U.S. Praises Duvalier for Democratic Commitment." Actually, the Duvaliers showed commitment to U.S. business interests, not democracy.

During the Duvalier family reign, an estimated 30,000 people were killed—with many more tortured or terrorized.

After Baby Doc was driven into exile in 1986, the U.S. still tried to have its way inside Haiti. In the country's first free presidential elections, in December 1990, the Bush White House threw its support behind a rich ex-official of the World Bank. The U.S.-backed candidate received 13 percent of the vote; activist priest Jean-Bertrand Aristide won in a landslide with 67 percent.

THE OBSTINATE ARISTIDE

President Aristide was scheduled to return to Haiti on Oct.

30 [1993]—under an agreement shaped by the U.S. and the United Nations. The Clinton administration spent months pressuring Aristide to make dangerous concessions to the military thugs who organized the September 1991 coup against his elected government.

Last June, near the end of negotiations for what became "the Governors Island Accord," news reports depicted Aristide as unduly reluctant to sign the pact—*which allows coup leaders to stay in the army.*

ARISTIDE THE NUT

Widely reported in recent weeks by journalists who've never seen the document, a CIA "psychological profile" (prepared during the Bush administration) portrays Aristide as mentally ill.

Clinton aides—and others who've seen President Aristide up close in office and in exile—dismiss the classified CIA dossier as a caricature written by analysts who despise the Haitian's leftist politics.

Yet the CIA profile is taken as gospel by some journalists. CBS-TV correspondent David Martin began his Oct. 13 report this way: "U.S. officials familiar with the psychological profile prepared by the CIA say Jean-Bertrand Aristide suffers emotional problems which require psychiatric treatment..."

The NAACP leadership has denounced such reports as "disinformation." Congressman Joe Kennedy complains about CIA rumor-mongering aimed at discrediting Aristide.

ARISTIDE THE HUMAN RIGHTS ABUSER

CBS correspondent Martin glibly reported that "during nearly eight months as president," Aristide "paid little mind to democratic principles." In fact, during his presidency a total of 19 political killings were documented in Haiti—with no evidence that any were approved or condoned by Aristide.

In contrast, according to a report by Americas Watch and other human rights groups, there were at least 76 political killings in Haiti during the 11 months before Aristide took

office. And since Aristide's ouster, several thousand civilians have been killed by the military and its allies.

Although critics claim Aristide encouraged lynchings of Duvalier allies, independent monitors say that the Aristide government brought about a big improvement in Haiti's human rights situation. "It is ludicrous to compare that progress with the systematic mass murder committed since by the army," says Kenneth Roth, executive director of Human Rights Watch.

News reports grossly distort reality when they suggest that Aristide's approach to human rights is somehow comparable to the brutality of Haiti's past or present rulers.

ARISTIDE THE "ANTI-AMERICAN"

Another common media theme came from CBS's David Martin: "Although he is living in the U.S. and counting on the Clinton administration to return him to power, Aristide has, at times, been virulently anti-American, once referring to the common enemy that is called the imperialist American."

As long as the history of U.S. support for Haitian dictators is kept out of the picture, such portraits of Aristide can make him seem irrationally hostile. The fact is that after becoming president, Aristide established good relations with the United States.

If Aristide is able to return to Haiti and resume his presidency without being killed, it will be a miracle. Almost as miraculous would be U.S. news coverage of Haiti containing forthright history.

October 27, 1993

Jimmy Carter and Human Rights: Behind the Media Myth

Jimmy Carter's reputation has soared lately.

Typical of the media spin was a Sept. 20 [1994] report on *CBS Evening News,* lauding Carter's "remarkable resurgence" as a freelance diplomat. The network reported that "nobody doubts his credibility, or his contacts."

For Jimmy Carter, the pact he negotiated in Haiti—which averted a military confrontation—is the latest achievement of his long career on the global stage.

During his presidency, Carter proclaimed human rights to be "the soul of our foreign policy." Although many journalists promoted that image, the reality was quite different.

Inaugurated 13 months after Indonesia's December 1975 invasion of East Timor, Carter stepped up U.S. military aid to the Jakarta regime as it continued to murder Timorese civilians. By the time Carter left office, about 200,000 people had been slaughtered.

Elsewhere, despotic allies—from Ferdinand Marcos of the Philippines to the Shah of Iran—received support from President Carter.

In El Salvador, the Carter administration provided key military aid to a brutal regime. In Nicaragua, contrary to myth, Carter backed dictator Anastasio Somoza almost until the end of his reign. In Guatemala—again contrary to enduring myth— major U.S. military shipments to bloody tyrants never ended.

After moving out of the White House in early 1981, Carter developed a reputation as an ex-president with a conscience. He set about building homes for the poor. And when he traveled to hot spots abroad, news media often depicted Carter as a skillful negotiator on behalf of human rights.

But a decade after Carter left the Oval Office, scholar James Petras assessed the ex-president's actions overseas—and found that Carter's image as "a peace mediator, impartial electoral observer and promoter of democratic values…clashes with the experiences of several democratic Third World leaders struggling against dictatorships and pro-U.S. clients."

From Latin America to East Africa, Petras wrote, Carter functioned as "a hard-nosed defender of repressive state apparatuses, a willing consort to electoral frauds, an accomplice to U.S. Embassy efforts to abort popular democratic outcomes and a one-sided mediator."

Observing the 1990 election in the Dominican Republic, Carter ignored fraud that resulted in the paper-thin victory margin of incumbent president Joaquin Balaguer. Announcing that Balaguer's bogus win was valid, Carter used his prestige to give international legitimacy to the stolen election—and set the stage for a rerun this past spring [1994], when Balaguer again used fraud to win re-election.

In December 1990, Carter traveled to Haiti, where he labored to undercut Jean-Bertrand Aristide during the final days of the presidential race. According to a top Aristide aide, Carter predicted that Aristide would lose, and urged him to concede defeat. (He ended up winning 67 percent of the vote.)

Since then, Carter has developed a warm regard for Haiti's bloodthirsty armed forces. Returning from his recent mission to Port-au-Prince, Carter actually expressed doubt that the Haitian military was guilty of human rights violations.

Significantly, Carter's involvement in the mid-September [1994] negotiations came at the urging of Lt. Gen. Raoul Cedras—who phoned Carter only days before the expected U.S. invasion and asked him to play a mediator role. (Cedras had floated the idea in an Aug. 6 appearance on CNN.)

Carter needed no encouragement. All summer he had been urging the White House to let him be a mediator in dealings with Haiti.

Carter's regard for Cedras matches his evident affection for Cedras' wife. On Sept. 20, back home in Georgia, Carter told a *New York Times* interviewer: "Mrs. Cedras was impressive, powerful and forceful. And attractive. She was slim and very attractive."

The day after American forces arrived in Haiti, President Clinton was upbeat, saying that "our troops are working with full cooperation with the Haitian military"—the same military he had described five days earlier as "armed thugs" who have "conducted a reign of terror, executing children, raping women, killing priests."

The latest developments in Haiti haven't surprised Petras, an author and sociology professor at Binghamton University in New York. When Carter intervenes, Petras said when we reached him on Sept. 20, "the outcomes are always heavily skewed against political forces that want change. In each case, he had a political agenda—to support very conservative solutions that were compatible with elite interests."

Petras described Carter as routinely engaging in "a double discourse. One discourse is for the public, which is his moral politics, and the other is the second track that he operates on, which is a very cynical realpolitik that plays ball with very right-wing politicians and economic forces."

With much of Haiti's murderous power structure remaining in place, the results are likely to be grim.

September 21, 1994

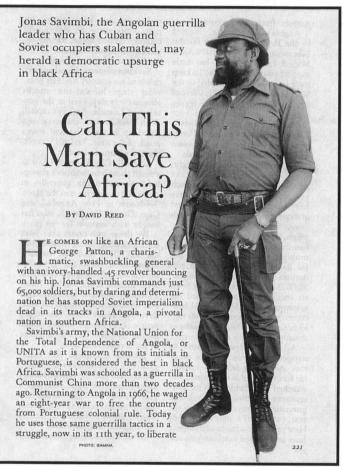

Jonas Savimbi, the Angolan guerrilla leader who has Cuban and Soviet occupiers stalemated, may herald a democratic upsurge in black Africa

Can This Man Save Africa?

BY DAVID REED

H E COMES ON like an African George Patton, a charismatic, swashbuckling general with an ivory-handled .45 revolver bouncing on his hip. Jonas Savimbi commands just 65,000 soldiers, but by daring and determination he has stopped Soviet imperialism dead in its tracks in Angola, a pivotal nation in southern Africa.

Savimbi's army, the National Union for the Total Independence of Angola, or UNITA as it is known from its initials in Portuguese, is considered the best in black Africa. Savimbi was schooled as a guerrilla in Communist China more than two decades ago. Returning to Angola in 1966, he waged an eight-year war to free the country from Portuguese colonial rule. Today he uses those same guerrilla tactics in a struggle, now in its 11th year, to liberate

PHOTO: GAMMA

221

U.S.-backed guerilla leader Jonas Savimbi, head of UNITA, hailed by May 1987 *Reader's Digest* as a democrat who "champions free enterprise."

Part XIII
Foreign Foes and Allies

News coverage of faraway events routinely takes the form of a morality play—with U.S.-backed supporters of "democracy," "reform" and "peace" juxtaposed against less virtuous forces. Between the lines of the media script, however, the situation tends to be quite different.

War on the Tube:
So Close Yet So Far Away

Television brings war into our living rooms. That's the conventional wisdom.

And so, we might be tempted to believe that news broadcasts with grisly footage from Bosnia or Rwanda make warfare real to us.

But the room where we sit in front of a TV set could hardly be farther from the realities of a war zone.

A war "is among the biggest things that can ever happen to a nation or people, devastating families, blasting away the roofs and walls," says media critic Mark Crispin Miller. But at home "we see it compressed and miniaturized on a sturdy little piece of furniture, which stands and shines at the very center of our household."

There's never any need to dig shrapnel out of the sofa. And while television "may confront us with the facts of death, bereavement, mutilation, it immediately cancels out the memory of that suffering, replacing its own pictures of despair with a commercial, upbeat and inexhaustibly bright."

But such limitations of the TV-viewing experience are only part of the problem with relying on television to understand the wars of the world. A bigger impediment is that some wars don't make it to the shimmering little box at all.

We're likely to assume that television is showing us the most horrendous and "important" wars. Yet news broadcasts are highly selective, for reasons that include political and racial biases.

Bloody events in Bosnia, for instance, have frequently dominated news programs. But we rarely hear a word, or see even a few seconds of videotape, about the war in Angola—where the victims are black Africans, and the United States government bears major responsibility for the carnage.

The rebel force known as Unita—long backed by U.S. officials who supplied massive aid—lost an internationally-supervised election to Angola's ruling party in 1992. Immediately, Unita launched a new military offensive. Since then, *half a million* Angolans have died, according to the British magazine *New Statesman*.

As the magazine reported in March [1994], the human suffering is immense in Angola: "Inexorably, month after month since the elections in September 1992, Unita's reign of terror has worsened, outstripping in horror the familiar scenes of starvation and factional or ethnic killing in Somalia, Liberia, Sudan, or Burundi. Yet this is a war the international community had the power to prevent."

The Unita killers owe a great deal to Western support. "First the Portuguese colonists, then the South Africans in pursuit of regional dominance, then the U.S. in the name of anti-communism created and nourished [Jonas] Savimbi and his Unita. This past two years have seen the United Nations appeasement compound" the tragedy.

But American media rarely discuss U.S. culpability or U.N. appeasement in Angola.

Writing in the *New Statesman*, journalist Victoria Brittain recalls: "Every year since the mid-1980s, I have interviewed dozens of displaced peasants who described attacks on their villages by Unita, kidnapping of young men and boys, looting, beatings, and killings, while in hospital beds the rows of mutilated women bore witness to the mining of their fields. Defectors from Unita told more chilling stories of mass rallies at the headquarters in Jamba where women were burned alive as witches. These were not stories the outside world wanted to hear about Unita, whose leader was regularly received at the White House."

The *New Statesman* article concludes: "Angola has been destroyed by Unita leader Jonas Savimbi's determination to take by force the power successive United States administrations promised him, but which the Angolan people denied him in the polls."

Since the election—rather than isolate Savimbi as the terrorist leader that he is—the U.S. and the United Nations have tried to placate him with concessions, more negotiations and access to material aid.

Meanwhile, the American news media tell us little about Angola—where the U.N. estimates that 1,000 people die each *day*.

Why don't we see Angola on the evening news? Or on the front pages?

Why have we seen so many stories about the Bosnian cities of Sarajevo and Gorazde, but none about the horrible sieges of Angolan cities like Cuito, Huambo and Malange?

For much the same reason that we rarely get any news about East Timor. Since December 1975, when Indonesia invaded that island nation and began to slaughter the native population, a protracted holocaust has been underway. More than 200,000 Timorese—a third of the entire population—have died at the hands of the occupiers.

The murderous Indonesian regime, allied with the U.S. government, has used American aircraft and other military aid to do the killing. Despite the U.S. link—or perhaps because of it—we haven't seen the massacres in East Timor on our TV screens.

We see news reports about the Kurds inside Iraq, suffering from the brutality of the Iraqi regime. But we rarely get news of the Kurds inside Turkey, suffering from the brutality of the Turkish regime.

Even when thousands of Turkish troops invade northern Iraq to attack Kurdish foes, as they did in mid-April, the event gets virtually no U.S. media coverage. Can you imagine the news coverage if Iraqi troops had invaded Turkey (a close U.S. ally) in pursuit of Kurdish guerrillas?

What we see on television only gives us fleeting glimpses of war. And the selectivity of those glimpses renders some victims invisible, their anguish ignored. Conveniently.

April 20, 1994

After the Mosque Bloodbath, Will Journalism Improve?

If a Palestinian had murdered 29 Israelis in a synagogue, major U.S. news outlets would have routinely described the gunman and his movement as "terrorist." Families of the Israeli victims would have been prominent in the news. Charts would have listed the history of attacks on Israeli civilians.

But when the murderer was an Israeli—Dr. Baruch Goldstein, an Army reserve officer and leader in the Kach extremist movement—reporters rarely used the word "terrorist." Some news accounts even seemed intent on justifying Goldstein's rage.

Families of the Palestinian victims were virtually invisible. Historical charts of prior, even bloodier, attacks on Palestinian civilians went unpublished—while several *New York Times* writers gave the impression that this was a first for violence against Palestinians.

Indeed, national media in the U.S. typically view Mideast violence from the Israeli perspective.

At the time of the Israeli-PLO peace agreement in September [1993], for example, PBS anchor Jim Lehrer repeatedly asked what would happen if, after Palestinian autonomy, a Palestinian attacked an Israeli. Lehrer expressed no concern about the many Palestinians assaulted by extremist Jewish settler groups that have long been coddled by Israeli courts.

With terrorism seen as a strictly Arab activity in much of the U.S. media, Israeli violence is often portrayed as "anti-terrorism." Palestinians murder, Israelis "retaliate."

While news reports on the mosque massacre [Feb. 25, 1994] generally failed to label Goldstein a *terrorist*, some had no trouble mentioning that Palestinian "terrorists" in the Hamas organization had killed two of Goldstein's friends from the Kiryat Arba settlement on Dec. 5 [1993]; Goldstein, we were told, may have been retaliating.

Unreported in most U.S. news accounts is the fact that, in the days before, armed vigilantes from Kiryat Arba—patrolling local roads with the blessing of Israeli soldiers—had gone on a shooting spree, killing a Palestinian. The Hamas killers said they were retaliating for these shootings.

It's no secret—except perhaps to Americans—that Israel's settler vigilantes harass unarmed West Bank Palestinians in a manner reminiscent of Ku Klux Klansmen in the old South. So proud are they of their intimidation tactics that Kiryat Arba thugs have allowed Israeli national TV to film their "road patrols."

In this endless cycle of violence, each atrocity is defended as "retaliation" against the other side's "terrorism." Journalists should reject such self-serving labels: either both sides' killing of civilians should be called *terrorism*, or neither.

The truth is that far more Palestinian civilians have been killed by the Israeli army and settlers than Israeli civilians slain by Palestinians.

And that doesn't include Palestinians killed by Israel's allies—as when 800 civilians were massacred in the Sabra and Chatila refugee camps, during Israel's 1982 invasion of Lebanon, by Christian Falangists who were allowed into the camps by Israeli soldiers.

Israel's aerial bombardment of Beirut in June of 1982 killed hundreds of Arab civilians day after day. As journalist Robert Fisk noted in *The Independent*, a British daily, reporters didn't call these air raids "terrorism," but rather, "military operations against 'terrorist targets.'"

Last July [1993], in "retaliation" for the killings of nine Israeli soldiers, Israel bombed Palestinian villages in southern Lebanon, killing over 100 civilians—intentionally leveling villages and creating many tens of thousands of refugees.

"As one of the few reporters in Lebanon at the time," wrote Fisk, "I watched women and children shrieking with pain in the hospital wards, their bodies plastered with burns from Israeli phosphorous shells."

Fisk continued: "This 'operation,' which killed so many

innocents, cost...$33 million, a bill that Washington helps to underwrite."

U.S. taxpayers—through billions of dollars in aid to Israel each year—have also helped to underwrite the occupation of the West Bank and Gaza Strip.

The brutal realities faced by Palestinians under occupation—although protested by many Israelis and documented in the Israeli press—are little understood in our country. Palestinians must pay taxes, but get few services and can't vote. They must carry I.D. cards, but must not carry weapons...despite the dangers from violent settlers.

Occupation soldiers—some sharing the racist attitudes of Israeli extremists—police the territories. By the thousands, Palestinian activists have been detained without trial, tortured or worse. Curfews are imposed as collective punishment.

Over the years, mainstream Israeli dailies have exposed Israel's confiscation of evermore Palestinian land and water for the exclusive use of the Jewish-settler minority, and have compared it to South African apartheid.

To this day, Palestinian families are being forcibly evicted from their homes, while settlements for Israelis—in state subsidized housing—are enlarged.

The Hebron mosque massacre has jarred a number of U.S. journalists into taking a closer look at the Israeli occupation. A better informed American public could exert pressure for a peace process built on justice.

March 2, 1994

U.S. Press Ignoring Israeli Prisoner

Six months have passed since a leading British newspaper launched its campaign to free a news source, who remains imprisoned under conditions that Amnesty International describes as "cruel" and "inhuman."

The newspaper is the *Sunday Times* of London. The source is a man named Mordechai Vanunu, now in his seventh year of solitary confinement inside a 7-by-10-foot cell in Israel.

So far the newspaper's campaign to free him—announced Nov. 29 [1992]—has gone unreported in major American news media.

Israel's government, which kidnapped Vanunu from Italy in September 1986 and has been holding him ever since, considers the former Israeli nuclear worker to be a treasonous spy.

But, as the *Sunday Times* editorialized in late 1992, "the Vanunu case is unique in one crucial respect: he was not a paid agent of a foreign power. Vanunu's 'crime' was to leak information to a newspaper—this newspaper. Should he remain alone in his cell until September 2004 for that?"

Right now that's the plan of Israeli authorities.

"All over the world," says *Sunday Times* editor Andrew Neil, "there is growing concern at the harshness of the charges and at the very long sentence imposed on Mordechai."

The Vanunu case continues to make headlines in Britain and elsewhere. But not here. With the exception of a *60 Minutes* segment on CBS early in this decade, the 1990s have been virtually Vanunu-free in the U.S. mass media.

For nine years Mordechai Vanunu worked as a technician at the Dimona complex in the Negev desert—where Israel has been producing nuclear warheads since the 1960s. To this day, however, the Israeli government sticks to the standard line that it "will not be the first to introduce nuclear weapons into the region."

The fiction of a nuclear-arms-free Israel is abetted by American officialdom. Using typical doubletalk two years ago, then-Secretary of Defense Dick Cheney declared on May 31, 1991: "As far as I know, Israel has never announced that it has any nuclear capability."

Meanwhile, Israel has proceeded with nuclear deployments. For instance, Seymour Hersh reports in his recent book *The Samson Option* that the Israeli military placed nuclear land mines along the Golan Heights in the early 1980s.

Washington regularly lectures—and threatens—countries such as Iraq and North Korea about the necessity of preventing the spread of nuclear weapons. But in its commitment to wink at Israel's stockpile of sophisticated nuclear weaponry, the U.S. government is obliged to turn a blind eye to the Vanunu case.

Born into a Jewish household in Morocco in 1954, Mordechai Vanunu and his family emigrated to Israel nine years later. After a three-year stint in the Israeli army, he began working at the Dimona nuclear plant in 1976.

In 1985, shortly before his employment ended at the nuclear facility, Vanunu secretly took photos inside Dimona, which has always been closed to international inspection. Using severance pay to travel abroad in 1986, he contacted the famed Insight investigative unit of Britain's *Sunday Times*, and flew to London.

"During his extensive debriefing by our Insight team," according to the *Sunday Times*, "he offered to give the paper his photographs and all his information for nothing provided we did not publish his name, insisting his sole interest was in stopping nuclear proliferation in the Middle East. It was explained that in order for his story to be believed he would have to be named and his credibility established."

Although the newspaper agreed to pay Vanunu for serialization or a book based on his information, staffers say he didn't seem to be after money.

"My impression of the man was of someone who had a genuine desire to tell the world of something that was going on which he felt was genuinely wrong for Israel to do," says Peter Hounam, the main reporter on the story for the *Sunday Times*. "He felt it was wrong that the Israeli public and parliament were not given any information about what was happening in Dimona."

On Oct. 5, 1986—under the front-page headline "REVEALED: THE SECRETS OF ISRAEL'S NUCLEAR ARSENAL"—the *Sunday Times* broke the story. But several days earlier, Vanunu had been kidnapped by Israel's intelligence service, the Mossad.

The newspaper later reported that Vanunu was lured by a female Mossad agent to Rome, "where he was attacked by two men and held down while she injected him with a powerful anaesthetic. He was chained and smuggled out of Italy in a cargo ship."

For several weeks the Israeli government interrogated Vanunu while denying any knowledge of what had happened to him. Then it announced that "Mordechai Vanunu is detained in Israel by law." Charging Vanunu with treason and espionage, Israel claimed he had returned to his country voluntarily.

But Vanunu wrote a contrary message on his palm, which he pressed to the window of a police van taking him to a court hearing in Jerusalem. His palm told the story: "Vanunu was hijacked in Rome, Italy, 30/9/86, 21:00 hours..." That's how the world learned he'd been kidnapped. (From then on, when transported to court, van windows were painted black.)

The press was barred from Vanunu's secret trial before an Israeli military court, which resulted in an 18-year prison sentence—his punishment for shedding light on Israel's arsenal of between 100 and 200 nuclear bombs.

Today, Vanunu remains in solitary confinement. "The longer he is kept in prison," the *Sunday Times* declared in a recent editorial, "the more he will become a martyr to the causes of press freedom and nuclear de-escalation."

In the United States, however, Vanunu stands little chance of becoming a martyr to the cause of press freedom. That's because the press keeps using its freedom to suppress his story.

[During 1994, major American news outlets continued to ignore Vanunu—despite new developments. A plea to end his imprisonment was signed by several former Middle East hostages, including journalists Terry Anderson and Charles

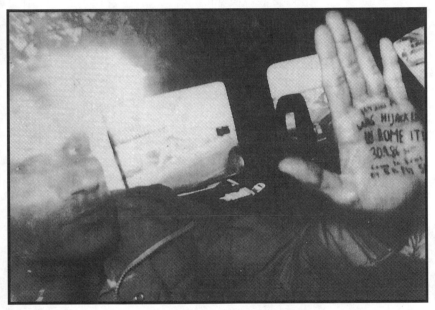

Mordechai Vanunu presses palm to the window of Israeli police van.

Glass. In April, Amnesty International called for Vanunu's immediate release. In October, he won the 1994 Sean McBride Peace Prize. And civil disobedience urging freedom for Vanunu occurred at Israeli diplomatic offices in seven U.S. cities.]

May 26, 1993

Missiles Deliver "Message"
as U.S. Press Ducks

Imagine waking up to news reports that began: "The CIA headquarters near Washington was struck by Cuban missiles last night, after Cuba cited 'compelling evidence' that the United States had plotted to assassinate its president.

"A statement released in Havana said the missile strike was aimed at 'sending a message' to the White House that plots against heads of state are unacceptable. Cuba called its action a 'firm and commensurate response'—and a 'success that minimized civilian casualties.'"

Imagine further that the news reports proceeded from beginning to end in this same matter-of-fact tone, offering no contradictory history, no dissenting views, no analysis of international law, no focus on the civilian victims, and no hint that a surprise missile attack against a capital city is a serious act of war that terrorizes its inhabitants.

If Washington had been attacked, such bloodless coverage would have been inconceivable. But when Washington does the attacking—as with its bombing of Baghdad [June 26, 1993] in response to Iraq's alleged plot to murder George Bush—such reporting is not only conceivable, but routine.

Here's some of what was missing from the coverage:

HISTORY

Our country's mainstream media buried the history of U.S. murder plots against foreign leaders—including close to ten different CIA plots to kill Cuba's Fidel Castro. According to intelligence memoirs and U.S. government documents (including the Senate's 1975-76 Church Committee reports), the CIA plotted the assassination or "removal" of Mossadegh of Iran, Nasser of Egypt, Lumumba of the Congo, Sukarno of Indonesia and many other heads of state.

In 1963, Bill Clinton's hero JFK gave the green light to

215

South Vietnamese generals to eliminate President Ngo Dinh Diem, who was then murdered. The CIA also helped overthrow several democratic governments by supporting military coups; in 1973, Chile's elected president, Salvador Allende, died in one of them.

Is there anyone sane who would justify missile assaults against Washington by any of these countries?

DISSENT

News outlets unanimously reported "bipartisan support in Congress" for President Clinton's action. What they didn't tell us is that Rep. Ronald Dellums, the chair of the House Armed Services Committee, issued a news release within hours of the missile attack asking how "an unrivaled superpower" can "presume to use unilateral military force to seek to vindicate the rule of international law." Dellums asked why the U.S. had not taken diplomatic action at the United Nations or legal action at the International Court of Justice.

Dellums asked good questions. Journalists provided no answers. Perhaps there's an obvious reason Clinton didn't take Iraq to the Court of Justice: In the 1980s, when that court convicted the U.S. of violating international law by mining Nicaragua's harbors and launching the Contra army to overthrow its government, the U.S. refused to recognize the court's jurisdiction. Washington might seem hypocritical to go to that court now.

"INTERNATIONAL LAW"

Unable or unwilling to use courts of law to get justice in the alleged Bush plot, the Clinton administration sought to cloak its missile attack in the language of international law. So it invoked Article 51 of the U.N. charter, which speaks of a country's "right to self-defense." Ironically, Washington last invoked this U.N. provision in 1986 when it tried to kill Libya's head of state in a bombing attack that missed Qaddafi but killed his young daughter.

National media offered almost no critical analysis of the

self-defense claim, but any first-year law student knows the difference between self-defense (force used to prevent an imminent attack or stop an ongoing attack) and retaliation (force used to avenge a past assault). In national or international law, there is no legal "right to retaliate," and no self-defense right to "send messages" to deter future attacks. The United Nations charter specifically forbids the use of force by one state against another, requiring the use of legal means like the Court of Justice or U.N. Security Council to resolve conflicts.

CIVILIAN VICTIMS

While U.S. news coverage didn't ignore the civilians who were killed or injured, they weren't focused on...or humanized. We didn't meet the victims' families or see their portraits. Instead, reporters continually recycled the administration line that the assault tactics were chosen to minimize civilian casualties—even though military planners know civilian deaths are unavoidable in such a massive missile attack. Indeed, after it was clear that residential neighborhoods had been barraged with missiles, the Pentagon insisted its mission had been a "success."

The day after the attack, a *New York Times* map—"Surveying the Damage in Baghdad"—pinpointed the 20 missiles that landed in the intelligence compound, but couldn't find room to show the three that hit residential neighborhoods nearby.

And journalists didn't seem to notice that the terrorism at the World Trade Center killed fewer civilians than U.S. "counter-terrorism" in Baghdad. Terrorism can be defined as committing violence against civilians to "send messages." Does the addition of the prefix "counter-" to "terrorism" exculpate those who send the bombs?

"ACT OF WAR"

The words "act of war" were not uttered by national news outlets, which preferred phrases like "sending Saddam a message," "retaliating against Hussein" or "punishing Saddam." The myth persists in U.S. media that terrifying missile attacks against a country may amount to little more than personal slaps

against a hated head of state. The myth helps us lose sight of the humanity of ordinary Iraqis.

If foreign missiles were falling on us, in retaliation for some bloody deed of the CIA, we might better understand the horror of living in Baghdad when a foreign power decides to "send a message."

[Within months of the missile attack on Baghdad, maverick reporters Seymour Hersh (in *The New Yorker*) and Patrick Cockburn (in *The Independent* and *In These Times)* had raised doubts about U.S. evidence of an Iraqi government murder plot against Bush.]

June 30, 1993

The Hero of America's TV News—Sheriff Yeltsin

Question: When is an autocrat a "democrat"?
Answer: When his name is Boris Yeltsin.

If you followed the early-autumn [1993] crisis in Moscow on American TV, the conflict was simple: Russian good guys (commanded by Yeltsin) defeated Russian bad guys (the "hard-liners").

On the day the standoff began, CBS anchor Dan Rather suggested that Yeltsin "didn't go far enough" months earlier in getting rid of the "hardliners." But how does a president legally get rid of elected members of parliament?

President Yeltsin did it by simply dissolving parliament on Sept. 21, a blatantly unconstitutional move that won immediate support from the Clinton administration.

Secretary of State Warren Christopher defended the power grab, borrowing from Orwell to applaud "President Yeltsin and his program of democratic reform." Soon after, the constitutional issue virtually dropped from view on American TV.

For the next 13 days, until the military assault on the Russian parliament, American TV served up a prolonged cowboy movie—featuring Sheriff Yeltsin against the outlaws.

While news reports spoke of negotiations between Yeltsin and "the hardline opposition," few noted Yeltsin's *hardline* refusal to agree to a presidential election simultaneous with new parliamentary elections—a compromise urged by the centrist Civic Union, Mikhail Gorbachev and others.

With the Clinton White House backing Yeltsin's every move, including ultimately the attack on Russia's "White House," American TV reporters abandoned even the pretense of objectivity.

Cable News Network doesn't air Westerns, but CNN was a place where Sheriff Yeltsin kept riding high. White hats were worn by "Yeltsin and the democratic movement"—black hats by "the hardliners."

CNN's postmortem on the storming of the parliament building, as reported by Walter Rogers, could have been scripted by Yeltsin's propaganda officers: "The Russian army was called to suppress an armed revolt led by hardline opponents trying to overthrow President Boris Yeltsin."

Throughout the crisis, the "hardline" tag begged for elucidation that never came.

Were they hardline Russian nationalists? The parliament speaker, Rulan Khasbulatov, is not even Russian. He's from the largely Muslim area of Chechnya.

Were they "old guard Communists," as ABC's Peter Jennings called them? In fact, they were Yeltsin's men. He hand-picked Khasbulatov to be his successor as parliament chairman when he ran for president. Then he chose Alexander Rutskoi as his vice presidential running-mate. Both Khasbulatov and Rutskoi were Communists for most of their lives—but so was Yeltsin, who served for years as the Communist mayor of Moscow.

One of TV's few dissenting voices was Stephen Cohen of Princeton University. While most network anchors and analysts were busy apologizing for the closing of the parliament and the attack on the building, Cohen offered something different—historical background:

The "hardline" leaders of parliament were elected in fairly free elections in 1990 near the end of the Gorbachev era. The leaders of parliament then defied Gorbachev and the Communist Party by first selecting Yeltsin as the chair of parliament, and then by amending the constitution so Yeltsin could run for the presidency of Russia.

During the 1991 coup by Communist diehards against Gorbachev, the parliament provided sanctuary to Yeltsin, helping to stave off the coup. A few months later, the parliament ratified Yeltsin's decision to abolish the Soviet Union, and then gave Yeltsin decree-making power for a year to institute his economic reforms. In a real sense, this had been Yeltsin's parliament.

With the Russian parliament building still in flames, American TV "experts" urged Yeltsin to prove his democratic credentials by pressing ahead with quick elections for a new legislative body. No one asked what might happen if the new parliament, like the old, falls out of favor with Yeltsin.

Other key questions also went unasked: If he is such a democrat, why wasn't Yeltsin willing to wait 18 months for the next scheduled parliamentary elections? Why does the new constitution—drafted by Yeltsin to replace the one he just abolished—give almost all power to the president, and almost none to the legislative branch?

And why does Yeltsin so dominate his country's TV—where most Russians get their news—that even a global figure like Gorbachev has been virtually banned?

Coverage also glossed over the economic forces tearing Russia apart.

At the behest of the World Bank and the International Monetary Fund—powerful institutions rarely scrutinized by U.S. media—the Yeltsin government has administered "shock treatment" to the Russian economy. As a result, most Russians are suffering new deprivations.

What used to be state property—including access to oil, precious metal and other natural resources—is being rapidly *privatized* and sold off to Western business interests. Hailed as "free-market economic reforms" by U.S. and Western European media, these policies enrich a few Russians while spurring corruption and economic chaos. Seniors watch their pensions disappear due to rampant inflation. Unemployment is rife.

From watching American television—where Russian critics of Yeltsinomics tend to be lumped with "hardliners"—you might not know that many Russian democrats oppose Yeltsin's "free-market reforms."

On the *MacNeil/Lehrer NewsHour*, co-anchor Margaret Warner anxiously asked a Russia expert whether he was sure that in future elections, "democrats and free marketeers would necessarily win?"

Although "democrat" and "free marketeer" are often

equated, the latter is more revered by the U.S. government and media pundits.

Recent events have shown that Boris Yeltsin is far more committed to privatization than democratization. And most of American mass media seem to share that preference.

October 6, 1993

Waist Deep in Big Russia's Economic Swamp

With the U.S. government escalating the Vietnam War in 1967, Pete Seeger penned the protest song: "Waist Deep in the Big Muddy, and the Big Fool Says to Push On." Although not named in the song, "the Big Fool" clearly referred to President Johnson.

The song could apply today to the deepening economic crisis in Russia. But who is "the Big Fool"?

No group is louder in urging a deeper push into the Big Muddy of Russian economic chaos than the U.S. press. Witness the grief expressed in mid-January [1994], when "free market" economist Yegor Gaidar—the commander of Russia's *shock therapy* transition to capitalism—resigned from Boris Yeltsin's cabinet. You'd have thought Mother Theresa had resigned from the Church.

When President Clinton departed Moscow a day earlier, U.S. media cheered him for pressuring Yeltsin to push on with economic shock therapy, and for a stellar performance on Moscow television reminding viewers of Russia's greatness.

If only the Russian people could subsist on a diet of inspirational words.

Lost in the media adulation of Clinton, Yeltsin and Gaidar was the fact that pushing the Russian economy deeper into fast-track privatization may well shock the Russian public into the arms of a fascist like Vladimir Zhirinovsky.

But you won't find much dissent over Russian economic policy in the U.S. press, which is so blinded by "free market" dogma that it can't comprehend the misery of average Russians.

In a Jan. 16 editorial, New York *Newsday* opposed any slowdown in "market reforms"—even objecting to the common-sense idea that Russia's economic transition should involve "less shock, more therapy."

Needless to say, the media pundits who issue such pronouncements are not worrying about their next meal.

You have to pity the poor Russians, though. After faring badly for decades in the hands of state-planning ideologues, their economic lives are now run by privatization ideologues.

When Clinton and the press plane flew from Moscow, they left behind a country in which one out of three people lives below subsistence level. Russia's 1992 plunge in consumer spending paralleled what happened in our country during the Great Depression. Meanwhile, inflation runs at more than 20 percent *a month*, making it almost impossible for pensioners and others to afford basic goods.

Production has ground to a halt in many areas. Unemployment grows. The health system has collapsed. Tuberculosis and diphtheria are spreading, while life expectancy declines.

Shock therapy is a bold theory. It calls for transforming a Communist state-run economy into a capitalist system within a couple of years—by suddenly ending price controls, privatizing state enterprises and resources, cutting public spending, and throwing open the country to foreign goods and investors.

As a pre-condition for getting financial aid and loans (most still undelivered) from the U.S., other Western governments and the International Monetary Fund, President Yeltsin implemented shock therapy—beginning in January 1992.

Two years later, the Russian economy is virtually destroyed—and according to Mikhail Gorbachev, a critic of Yeltsinomics, Russians don't "see light at the end of the tunnel."

Perhaps it's time for the austerity pundits and privatization true-believers to curb their dogma—and grasp the dreadful realities brought on by their beloved theory.

This is not to say that everyone is a loser in today's Russia. Some Western interests (and their Russian partners) are benefiting—as they gain access to Russia's raw materials at fire-sale prices. And corrupt government officials, some close to Yeltsin, get rich by authorizing the export of oil or precious metals to this or that foreign company.

Russian capitalism has also spawned a powerful local

"Mafia"—which bribes government officials to facilitate dealings in drugs and prostitution, protection rackets, and illegal exports of raw materials.

The wealth of Russia's unsavory "New Rich" is widely seen as deriving from foreign interests and a foreign system. In a country where most people are suffering, these inequities provide fodder for the ravings of racists and xenophobes like Zhirinovsky.

December's election, which made Zhirinovsky's party the biggest in the parliament, was a massive rejection of economic shock therapy.

Most U.S. media downplayed this point, and are now content to reduce Russian politics to a standoff between Yeltsin and Zhirinovsky—with no other options.

But there *are* other options. Many Russian parties, intellectuals, economic managers and union leaders are calling for an end to shock therapy and a slowdown in the move toward a market economy so that workers, pensioners and industries can be protected.

Maybe these folks would get more attention in U.S. media if they started singing "Waist Deep in the Big Muddy."

Or maybe not. The song was suppressed—during the Johnson era—by American broadcast networks.

January 19, 1994

Mexico's Election:
A Triumph for Media Spin

Soon after Mexico's ruling Institutional Revolutionary Party (PRI) claimed victory, we reached journalist John Ross in Mexico City and asked for his impression of the U.S. press corps that had crossed the Rio Grande to cover the election. The laughter on the phone line was dry as desert sand.

"They know a couple of Mexicans," he said. "They know their maid. They know their taxi driver. And they know their inside source within the PRI structure that's constantly feeding them the most self-serving information.... The point is that they have no contact with the *pueblo*."

Ross has reported from the cities and remote villages of Mexico for most of the last two decades; during the presidential election six years ago, he was the *San Francisco Examiner* correspondent there. In recent months he has been writing about Mexico for such periodicals as the weekly *San Francisco Bay Guardian* and *The Nation* magazine.

In mid-August [1994], when foreign observers arrived in Mexico City to monitor the election, Ross accepted an invitation to brief the group. "I told them to go home."

Why? "Basically the fraud has taken place since 1988, and the foreign observers are just here to legitimize the quantification of the fraud generated in the blood of the opposition and the lies of the ruling party."

The U.S. media framed the Aug. 21 election story as a matter of whether the balloting would be "free and fair"—with little reference to what happened in the months and years that led up to election day.

During the past six years, according to Ross, political killings in Mexico have taken the lives of 256 active supporters of the opposition Democratic Revolutionary Party, whose presidential candidate Cuauhtemoc Cardenas lost the election to blatant vote-counting fraud in 1988. Those killings rarely rated even a back-page mention in the U.S. press.

Meanwhile, ongoing theft of local elections kept PRI officials in powerful positions. The patronage system of the PRI—which has ruled Mexico for 65 years in a row—distributed payola to people in villages and urban slums as the latest election neared. And Ernesto Zedillo, now the president-elect, also benefitted from the PRI's enormous advantage in campaign funds—along with overwhelming favoritism from the nation's biggest TV outlets.

"On a day in early June when Cardenas drew 30,000 at the Autonomous University in southern Mexico City," recalls Ross, "the country's top newscaster, Televisa's Jacobo Zabludovsky, glossed over the huge rally and featured a 25-minute interview with Zedillo."

This year, the U.S. government maintained a public posture of non-involvement. An Aug. 14 *New York Times* headline described Washington's role in the election campaign as "Hands Off: In Mexico, U.S. Hones Art of Laissez-Faire Diplomacy." Yet the U.S. Embassy in Mexico City was very active. In July, Ross recounts, it flew in a select group of prestigious U.S. journalists to help orient their coverage.

As soon as the election was over, network TV news shows—from the PBS *MacNeil/Lehrer NewsHour* to *NBC Nightly News*—had U.S. Ambassador James Jones explaining what it all meant. Not surprisingly, the ambassador pronounced the elections a democratic triumph.

When other U.S. observers had something else to say, they were apt to be ignored or misrepresented. Medea Benjamin, head of a 115-member delegation organized by the San Francisco group Global Exchange, announced findings of fraud the day after the election at a Mexico City press conference. Yet many news dispatches declared that foreign observers had judged the elections clean. NPR's *All Things Considered* reported that visiting Sen. John McCain (R-Ariz.) said the election had been fair—and, NPR added, "that was pretty much the consensus of the American observers here."

Meanwhile, Civic Alliance—a nonpartisan coalition of

Mexican groups with funding from the United Nations—drew on data from its 12,000 poll-watchers, documenting a wide array of what many U.S. news stories euphemistically called "irregularities." Alliance Coordinator Enrique Calderon said: "These were definitely not clean elections."

A common media rationale for downplaying the significance of fraud was that presidential winner Zedillo ran well ahead of his nearest rivals. Yet congressional seats in both houses—not just the presidency—hung in the balance, and more than a few were apparently decided by fraud.

Two days after the election, a *New York Times* editorial acknowledged "embarrassing incidents"—but argued that "preliminary figures suggest so wide a margin for Mr. Zedillo...that hanky-panky is unlikely to have affected the outcome."

"Hanky-panky"? Even the same *New York Times* editorial noted a few of the problems: "Some people could not get ballots. Others complained that voting secrecy had been compromised. Independent monitors reported instances of multiple voting." Not exactly minor pranks.

Electoral abuses were widespread, Civic Alliance monitors found: At 24 percent of the voting stations, unlisted persons were allowed to vote; at 37 percent of the polling stations, balloting was not secret; thousands of Mexicans with proper credentials were refused ballots.

Overall, U.S. media missed key layers of the Mexico story—the contrast between the country's thin varnish of privilege and vast grinding poverty. In recent years, a wave of privatization championed by the PRI—and widely lauded in U.S. media as economic "reform"—has ripped big holes in longtime safety nets of social services and food subsidies for the poor.

Much of the PRI's huge bankroll for the election campaign came from wealthy beneficiaries of recent sell-offs of state resources to industrialists. The PRI government's economic program, John Ross reports, "has given Mexico 24 billionaires and 15 million people in extreme poverty."

But for many U.S. media outlets, when it comes to Mexico, the bottom line seems to be, well, the bottom line. In its wrap-up coverage of the election results, *NBC Nightly News* concluded on an upbeat note: "All of this is good news for U.S. investors."

August 24, 1994

Part XIV
Behold the Global Marketplace

The overall media tenor has been adulatory—heralding a "free trade" extravaganza sparked by NAFTA and GATT. Less publicized, the International Monetary Fund and the World Bank also have huge impacts across the planet. The emerging economic order is glorious...except for its many casualties.

Putting Free Trade Ahead
of a Free Press

Our country's most influential daily, the *New York Times*, has long claimed to cover the news "without fear or favor." But if you saw the *Times* business section on July 21 [1993], you saw that paper tilting in favor of one side in a national debate.

Labor unions were so upset by the bias that they set up informational picket lines at the newspaper's headquarters in New York, and *Times* bureaus in seven other cities.

The protests were sparked by a seven-page "advertorial" that combined ads with simulated news articles and columns, all harmoniously singing the praises of the North American Free Trade Agreement—the controversial pact that would open up investment and trade across the Mexican border.

It's hard to imagine the *Times* bestowing a seven-page package on one side in the abortion, gun-control or gays-in-the-military debates. But in the NAFTA controversy, the *Times* has granted "most-favored" treatment to the corporate side.

In the coming months, NAFTA is likely to embroil the country in a rancorous debate. But there was little rancor in the *NewYork Times* NAFTA section, and no debate. The *Times* adamantly refused to accept articles, or even paid ads, from anyone opposing NAFTA.

So readers of the *Times* did not hear from NAFTA critics who say the "free trade" agreement is costly—in lost jobs and degraded environment. Critics say NAFTA will speed the exodus of U.S. investment and jobs toward border-area industrial plants in Mexico—"maquiladoras"—employing low-paid labor in often unsafe conditions, and spewing out toxics that pollute both sides of the border.

NAFTA is opposed by many U.S. labor unions, the National Rainbow Coalition, Public Citizen (founded by Ralph Nader), and environmental groups including the Sierra Club, Greenpeace and Friends of the Earth. None of them was allowed to take out ads or contribute a word to the *Times* supplement.

By offering its pages exclusively to U.S. and Mexican companies that stand to profit from NAFTA—like AT&T and SkyTel—the *New York Times* grossed an estimated $200,000.

The package contained columns extolling NAFTA by Treasury Secretary Lloyd Bentsen and Sen. Bill Bradley, a piece on how NAFTA will bolster the economies of various states, and a newsy item reporting that "special interest groups—most notably labor and environmental—have funded and organized their attempts to derail the agreement very well."

When we called the *New York Times* to get its explanation, the paper's spokesperson stressed that the word "Advertisement" appeared in top corners of each page, and that a small print disclaimer said the supplement "did not involve the reporting or editing staff of the *New York Times*."

But we've obtained a letter that the *Times* sent to companies soliciting their ad dollars to underwrite the pro-NAFTA section. "In an effort to educate the public and influence Washington decision makers," the letter stated, "the *New York Times* has planned a series of special advertorials presenting the positive economic and social benefits of NAFTA."

According to the letter, the *Times'* pro-NAFTA supplement would address the "many Americans [who] require further understanding if they are to be supportive of free trade…"

The best way a newspaper can promote "understanding" of an issue is with in-depth reporting—not a profit-making scheme that chooses sides.

In its editorials, the *Times*—like other national dailies—has been unabashedly pro-NAFTA. Big media outlets are frequently owned by multinational corporations that profit from "free trade" policies. The *Times*, for example, benefits as a result of its ownership interest in Canadian paper mills.

For many years, the *New York Times* has maintained an editorial posture that often equates what's good for the country with what's good for business: deregulation, free trade, standing tough against unions, etc.

And now there's the advertorial promotion of NAFTA.

It's ironic that only nine days earlier, on July 12, the *New York Times* front page featured the results of a *Times* poll under the headline: "Free Trade Pact Is Still a Mystery To Many in U.S.: Accord's Public Support Is Weak, Poll Shows." The story reported that while 22 percent favor NAFTA, and 23 percent oppose it, almost half (49 percent) of U.S. citizens say they know nothing about the trade pact—which the *Times* reporter described, accurately, as "a sweeping package of economic changes."

Given the extent of ignorance about such an important topic, a newspaper truly committed to covering the issues "without fear or favor" might have published a special section of solid journalism, not just advertorials limited to one point of view.

Of course there's an economic advantage to the *New York Times* approach: Journalism requires that reporters be paid. When it comes to one-sided propaganda, politically-minded corporations will foot the bill.

July 21, 1993

Mass Media Slanted the Debate in Behalf of NAFTA

In theory, the biases of newspaper owners and publishers are confined to editorials, while the rest of the paper is fair and objective. This theory has been clearly refuted in the case of NAFTA—endorsed almost unanimously by media owners and other corporate managers.

Although no editorial page has been more staunchly pro-NAFTA than the *Wall Street Journal*, its reporters are supposed to be "objective." Yet a *Journal* reporter asserted, during a TV interview two weeks before the House vote, that an upswing in poll support for NAFTA showed "things are moving in the right direction."

The scientific way to analyze the bias of news reporting is to scrutinize the sources and experts that reporters rely on. That's what our associate Jim Naureckas did in a four-month study of the country's two most influential papers—the *New York Times* and *Washington Post*. The study showed news coverage slanted in favor of NAFTA.

Of the 201 total sources quoted in the two papers from April through July [1993], only six (3 percent of the total) were environmentalists. Not one representative of a labor union was quoted during the four months—although one person was quoted from a coalition that includes unions. Members of the public who would be affected by the pact were virtually invisible.

Who *did* get to speak in the *Times* and the *Post*? Most of the sources (51 percent) were U.S. government officials—overwhelmingly pro-NAFTA. Another 13 percent were corporate representatives, even more overwhelmingly supporting the pact. And 11 percent were foreign government officials—mainly Mexican and Canadian—also heavily pro-NAFTA.

Adding it all up, NAFTA supporters outnumbered opponents by more than three to one.

Besides the ability to slant debate, news outlets have the power to turn reality upside down by claiming the debate is slanted the other way.

What prompted our study was the whining from major media about the unfairness of the NAFTA debate. The *New York Times* reported in August [1993] that business was stepping up its pro-NAFTA efforts "after months of letting unions and environmental groups dominate the debate." Yet those groups had been virtually excluded from *Times* news coverage.

In May, with a typical lack of evidence, *Washington Post* columnist Hobart Rowen proclaimed that "most of the voices being heard on the trade treaty, including those of labor union leaders and former presidential candidates Jerry Brown and Ross Perot, are solidly anti-NAFTA."

When Sen. Byron Dorgan (D-N.D.), a NAFTA foe, conducted his own column-inch count of editorial and op-ed articles appearing in the *Washington Post* this year, he found that the pro-pact bias was nearly seven to one. (Other papers were even more lopsided.) The senator wrote up his findings in a column, "Getting a Word in Edgewise on NAFTA"—but the *Post* wouldn't print it.

The pro-corporate bias of most mainstream media has been glaring in NAFTA coverage ever since the presidential campaign.

During the primaries, when candidate Bill Clinton's support for NAFTA seemed to waver briefly, commentators asked whether Clinton is "too controlled by big labor"—a mortal sin to the pundit elite. Yet not one mainstream pundit questioned Clinton's pro-NAFTA stance as evidence that he's "too controlled by big business."

In national media, the pundit spectrum excludes regular commentators who advocate for labor or the environment. Michael Kinsley, who supposedly represents "the left" on CNN, is so vehement in support of NAFTA that he once argued—nonsensically—that U.S.-owned plants in Mexico pay workers in dollars, and that "you can only spend them in the United States."

Anthony Lewis, the syndicated columnist who has represented the "left wing" of the *New York Times* for years, recently touted NAFTA by pillorying U.S. labor unions like the United Auto Workers for seeking to protect middle-class manufacturing jobs—which Lewis dismissed as largely "low-wage jobs." He attacked the "crude threatening tactics used by unions" in lobbying against NAFTA.

With labor-bashing intensifying in the media, President Clinton picked up the cudgel on the Nov. 7 *Meet the Press*, where he denounced unions for pressuring Congress with "roughshod, musclebound tactics." In the next breath, Clinton complained that pro-NAFTA business owners "have not gotten their employees and rank-and-file people to call and say they're for it." No pundit pointed out how "roughshod" it can be for management to pressure workers to support its political positions.

For months, news reports trivialized NAFTA opposition by referring to the "strange bedfellows" or "bizarre coalition" of critics: Ross Perot, Patrick Buchanan, Jesse Jackson, Ralph Nader. Only occasionally did coverage mention the oddball alliance in support of NAFTA—which unites Clinton and many liberals with the likes of Rush Limbaugh, George Will and Newt Gingrich.

Media decisions helped make Ross Perot the most visible NAFTA critic—despite the TV networks' refusal to air his anti-NAFTA infomercials. (NBC has sold Perot air time for messages it doesn't oppose, like deficit-reduction.)

Long before Perot became a household word, coalitions of environmental and labor groups were rallying the public against NAFTA. Their spokespersons are articulate *and* factual—but were rarely allowed on primetime.

On the very day Al Gore challenged Perot to debate, Ralph Nader—who has credibility with middle-class consumers—criticized NAFTA with eloquence and detail at a National Press Club news conference. But unless you saw Nader on C-SPAN, you probably never heard about it.

Many of NAFTA's leading critics see the issue as one of

corporate accountability: the need to restrain the power of multinational corporations that owe allegiance only to their bottom line—not to communities, workers or the environment.

Instead of folksy soundbites from Ross Perot, what our country needs is a serious debate on corporate flight from commitments to the public.

November 10, 1993

After NAFTA, Here Comes GATT…
The Stealth Pact

Approval of the North American Free Trade Agreement was a messy process. But at least it was a process—and the whole world was watching.

To win in Congress last November [1993], the White House doled out so much pork that the Rose Garden resembled a pig auction—while a largely pro-NAFTA press winked and held its nose.

To gain the votes of Florida congressmembers, the White House wrote to Florida fruit growers assuring them that they could keep using a dangerous ozone-depleting pesticide. To secure a Texan's vote, the administration said it would place a federally-funded lab in his district to explore the "positive side of plutonium."

Although the media debate was imbalanced—with pro-NAFTA voices dominating news reports and commentary—at least there was a debate.

That can't be said about a more earth-shaking pact signed in mid-April [1994] by over 100 countries in Morocco. The General Agreement on Tariffs and Trade has received remarkably little media coverage and virtually no debate—even though Congress has held countless hearings on the agreement.

Most of GATT's scant news coverage has amounted to cheerleading.

In December 1993, GATT spent two days in the news when U.S. and European officials concluded a seven-year round of negotiations—the so-called "Uruguay Round."

A front-page story in the *New York Times* began this way: "Free trade means growth. Free trade means growth. Free trade means growth. Just say it 50 more times and all doubts will melt away." It seemed like satire, but the one-sided article—headlined "How Free Trade Prompts Growth: A Primer"—did little more than quote economists singing the praises of "free trade."

And it was no joke when ABC's Peter Jennings introduced a report inquiring into what GATT "means for the U.S."—which allowed only one person to answer: Trade Representative Mickey Kantor, the man who'd negotiated for the United States.

Kantor's response: "Jobs. Wealth. Increased standard of living. Growing capital. More profits." (He forgot to promise "eternal life.")

There are opposing views on GATT. You just don't hear them much in the mass media. When Ralph Nader and Public Citizen recently unveiled a detailed study showing how GATT could undermine U.S. food safety standards, the press yawned.

Consumer rights groups strongly oppose GATT, and have joined with unions and others in the Citizens Trade Campaign. Key environmental groups—including several that supported NAFTA—are also in opposition. GATT doesn't even recognize the meager environmental and labor safeguards contained in NAFTA "side agreements."

Launched in 1948, GATT negotiations initially were aimed at reducing tariffs. But critics say that the recent Uruguay Round—propelled by Reagan-era deregulation mania—became a power play by multinational corporations to weaken the authority of national legislative bodies in protecting consumers, workers and the environment.

Critics fear GATT would usher in a New World Corporate Order by establishing an unaccountable, secretive World Trade Organization—similar in authority to the United Nations, but without giving nations any votes—that could jeopardize democratically-enacted laws.

GATT will reduce not just tariffs, but also so-called "non-tariff trade barriers"—allowing the World Trade Organization to rule against health and safety inspections, environmental laws, farm subsidies, etc.

GATT tribunals have already obliged Thailand to lift its ban on tobacco imports, and ruled in favor of Mexico when it challenged the U.S. dolphin protection law as an "illegal barrier" to Mexico's ability to sell us tuna.

The European Union is currently using GATT to challenge

U.S. auto fuel economy standards as a barrier to gas guzzlers. Europe says other "trade barriers" include the U.S. Consumer Nutrition and Education Labeling Act, and state recycling laws. Under the new GATT, if a U.S. law is declared a trade barrier, the United States would have to change the law or pay perpetual trade penalties.

Although signed by more than 100 countries, the Uruguay Round was driven by giant companies based in the wealthiest nations. A vice president of the huge Cargill agribusiness firm drafted the GATT provisions deregulating agriculture—which have sparked protests by family farmers in many countries, and riots by farmers in India.

Ralph Nader denounces GATT and the "megacorporations" that secretly helped negotiate it. Testifying before Congress, he argued: "The Fortune 200's GATT agenda would make the air you breathe dirtier and the water you drink more polluted. It would cost jobs, depress wage levels and make workplaces less safe. It would destroy family farms and make the food you eat contaminated with bacteria and pesticides and preservatives."

Nader's testimony didn't get any major media attention.

GATT could empower big corporations to undermine laws in closed hearings, at the global level, that they could not defeat in open debate in state legislatures or Congress.

It comes down to a conflict between big business and democracy. Judging from news coverage of GATT, major media outlets are siding with big business.

April 13, 1994

Media Whitewash Harm
Done By Global Loan Sharks

We rarely hear about them in the major news media—and when we do, we get mostly fluff and flackery.

According to the media image, they function tirelessly to encourage "reforms" so that backward countries can get their economic houses in order.

Who are they? The International Monetary Fund and the World Bank—the two most powerful financial institutions on earth.

From Russia and Thailand to Bolivia and Chile, the IMF and the World Bank provide loans—and constant advice. Well-heeled economists from affluent countries routinely offer billions of dollars, *if* the needy nations prove willing to make certain changes in policies.

Serving as a conduit for money from Western governments and banks and bondholders (with the United States as the biggest single source of funds), the IMF and World Bank require that recipient nations adhere to strict "structural adjustment" programs. They include easing limits on foreign investment, increasing exports, suppressing wages, cutting social services such as health care and education, and keeping the state out of potentially profitable endeavors.

"The World Bank and the IMF don't just have direct control over tens of billions of dollars per year," points out researcher Kevin Danaher of the Global Exchange organization based in San Francisco. "They also indirectly control much more from the commercial banks by functioning as a good housekeeping seal of approval. Offending governments who won't follow IMF/World Bank prescriptions get cut off from international lending—no matter how well those governments may be serving their own people."

In Africa, Asia and Latin America, the pattern has been grim: To get grants and loans, governments agree to devalue currencies and cut subsidies—thus raising the prices of necessities like food—while freezing wages and reducing public employment. Scores of countries are struggling to pay the interest on old loans and qualify for new ones.

The spiral has brought deepening poverty and debt. "From the onset of the debt crisis in 1982, until 1990, debtor countries paid creditors in the North $6,500 million [$6.5 billion] per month in interest alone," reports the British magazine *New Scientist*. "Yet in 1991 those countries were 61 percent more indebted than they were in 1982."

While the U.S. press is apt to portray the IMF and World Bank as selfless Good Samaritans, the reality is that these 50-year-old institutions function more like global loan sharks. One way countries are encouraged to repay their debts is by shifting from domestic agriculture to export crops.

Davison Budhoo, an economist who resigned from the IMF in protest, contends that the agency's approach has "led to the devastation of traditional agriculture, and to the emergence of hordes of landless farmers in virtually every country where the World Bank and IMF operate." And, he adds, "Food security has declined dramatically in all Third World regions, but in Africa in particular."

In Zimbabwe—formerly known as the breadbasket of Southern Africa—the IMF pressured the nation's Grain Marketing Board to make a profit by selling much of its stockpiled grain. And the U.S. Agency for International Development encouraged Zimbabwe to grow high-grade tobacco. As a result, acreage for corn dropped sharply—and the specter of famine was not far behind.

A disaster for all concerned? Not quite. Such disasters in the Southern Hemisphere have a way of serving as bonanzas for bankers in the North. Interest payments keep flowing northward as debt burdens increase.

Since 1980, "structural adjustment" has been visited upon more than 70 countries. "There are losers and there are winners in structural adjustment," says Leonor Briones, president of the Freedom from Debt Coalition in The Philippines. "The losers are those who are already losing. The winners: the banks, the businessmen, the politicians."

The international affairs director of the D.C.-based Environmental Defense Fund, Bruce Rich, cites the World Bank's "sad record of supporting military regimes and governments openly violating human rights." And he points to environmentally destructive actions such as last summer's approval of a $400 million World Bank loan to India for coal-burning power plants—anathema to those concerned about global warming and CO_2 emissions.

A revealing memo by the World Bank's chief economist, Lawrence Summers, was leaked in January 1992: "The economic logic behind dumping a load of toxic waste in the lowest wage country is impeccable, and we should face up to that.... I've always thought that underpopulated countries in Africa are vastly under-polluted." (Summers went on to become the Clinton administration's undersecretary of the treasury for international affairs.)

In his new book *Utopia Unarmed*, the Mexican scholar Jorge Castaneda calls the World Bank and the IMF "the institutions that play the most important role in managing international economic relations today." Yet the U.S. mass media tell us little about these agencies casting enormous fiscal shadows across the globe.

Raising questions about the International Monetary Fund and the World Bank could provoke far-reaching responses. As political analyst Noam Chomsky has put it: "To challenge the right of investors to determine who lives, who dies, and how they live and die—that would be a significant move toward Enlightenment ideals.... That would be revolutionary."

February 9, 1994

Compassion for Children
Gets Lost in Big Numbers

The death of one child can be big news. But the deaths of a million children are rarely news at all.

Sometimes, when a child suffers, the news media convey painful realities in human terms. We keep seeing pictures, and hearing from loved ones. And the entire nation seems to grieve.

That's what happened a couple of months ago, when the hunt for 12-year-old Polly Klaas ended with the awful discovery of her lifeless body. The front pages and network news told of her ordeal in excruciating detail. Later, President Clinton mentioned her by name in his State of the Union speech.

Around the world, every day about 35,000 young children die—not after being kidnapped, but after being held in a different kind of bondage: poverty.

Despite all the high-tech global communications systems, we find out little about those children. Reported as dry statistics, or not reported at all, the *preventable* deaths of several hundred thousand kids each month seem far less tragic than the well-publicized deaths of a few children.

Millions of kids are dying each year, the United Nations Children's Fund (UNICEF) declared recently, because the task of keeping them alive is low on the agendas in powerful offices: "The job is not being given sufficient priority because those most seriously affected are the poorest and least influential people on earth."

That description largely explains why the news media in our country—obsessed with the lifestyles of the rich and famous—don't tell us much about the suffering of children on this planet. When UNICEF released its report titled "The State of the World's Children 1994," the grim facts got only fleeting media coverage.

"Ordinary malnutrition and disease kill nearly 13 million children a year and leave millions more with poor growth and ill health," UNICEF reported. "It is a tragedy that rarely makes the news—because it is not exceptional."

Not exceptional, but often preventable.

Each year, almost 3 million children die from diarrhea. Yet the fatal dehydration can be prevented with a cheap oral solution of salts and sugars.

Lack of Vitamin A causes blindness in a quarter-million children each year—and, UNICEF adds, "is a major cause of ill health and early death among the world's under-fives. Again, there is a relatively simple solution. If diets cannot be altered to include more of the green leafy vegetables that are rich in Vitamin A, then Vitamin A capsules can be given to all children at risk for a cost of only a few cents per child."

And a pinch of iodized salt would make an enormous difference for huge numbers of children. "The human body needs only a teaspoonful of iodine in a whole lifetime," says UNICEF. But when mothers lack iodine, "at least 30,000 babies are stillborn every year, and over 120,000 are born as cretins—mentally retarded, physically stunted, deaf-mute or paralyzed."

The solution is readily available: "Everyone eats salt in some form—so iodizing all salt supplies can eliminate iodine deficiency quickly and cheaply. Within a year of all salt being iodized, no more cretins are born and goitres begin to shrink."

"With a major push now," UNICEF says, deficiencies of Vitamin A and iodine "could be overcome by the end of 1995."

While news media in the United States tend to portray impoverished Third World countries as sinking under the weight of despotism or "tribalism," UNICEF points out that the current situation is profitable for some in the West, especially lending institutions: "Africa spends more on debt repayment than on its health and education services. The continent is being exploited in its hour of need, and the heaviest consequences are falling on Africa's children."

Nor are the threats to children only overseas. Twenty-one countries—including South Korea, Singapore and Spain—have a lower mortality rate for children under age 5 than the U.S. does. Meanwhile, the overall poverty rate for children is twice as high here as in any other industrialized nation.

UNICEF reports some progress in the battle against childhood diseases around the world. In the past ten years, for instance, the annual death toll from measles has dropped from 2.5 million to about 1 million. The annual number of children crippled by polio has gone from a half-million to 140,000 during the last dozen years.

When UNICEF released its "State of the World's Children 1994" report at a White House news conference with President Clinton in late December [1993], the U.N. agency led off with this statement: "The world's long-term problems of poverty, population growth, and environmental deterioration will not be overcome without stepping up the effort to end malnutrition, illiteracy and disease among the world's children."

Some newspapers, however, decided to go with upbeat headlines. "Dramatic Gains Against Child Diseases Told," said the front-page *Los Angeles Times* headline. The *Washington Post* chose for its Page One headline, "Child Deaths From Disease on Decline Worldwide."

In contrast, on the same day, the *Chicago Tribune* conveyed the urgent message of the U.N. report with a front-page headline: "Cold War Still Hurts World's Kids; Even U.S. Youngsters Suffer, UNICEF Says." And the St. Louis *Post-Dispatch* headline read: "Developing Nations Beat U.S. in Child Care, UNICEF Says."

"We need to wake up," says Sam Harris, the executive director of RESULTS, a grassroots hunger-lobbying organization. "We have a measles vaccine, but 1 million children still die each year from this childhood killer. We have ORT, a simple gatorade-like solution that could save half of the 3 million children who die every year from dehydration due to diarrhea. These children die for lack of attention, our attention, governments' attention. They die not because they have to, but because saving their lives is not a priority."

Like many other activists, Harris is critical of news media priorities: "If today's headlines and soundbites are any indication, our new technology will only serve to feed us more sex and mindless mayhem…. If we cannot focus, we will have no vision."

January 26, 1994

Part XV
The Media Beat Goes On

The U.S. media landscape offers an array of Orwellian features. Some of the hyped-up terrain may seem laughable, but the overall effects are dead serious. "For those who stubbornly seek freedom," says Noam Chomsky, "there can be no more urgent task than to come to understand the mechanisms and practices of indoctrination."

George Orwell's Unhappy 90th Birthday

George Orwell would have reached his 90th birthday on June 25 [1993]. The great English writer has been dead for several decades, but Orwellian language lives on.

These days we have plenty of good reasons to echo poet W.H. Auden: "Oh, how I wish that Orwell were still alive, so that I could read his comments on contemporary events!"

Today, in the United States, media coverage of political discourse attests to Orwell's observation that language "becomes ugly and inaccurate because our thoughts are foolish, but the slovenliness of our language makes it easier for us to have foolish thoughts."

Anyone who pays attention to routine speeches by politicians is likely to recognize Orwell's description: "When one watches some tired hack on the platform, mechanically repeating the familiar phrases...one often has a curious feeling that one is not watching a live human being but some kind of dummy."

News media frequently make things worse. Instead of scrutinizing the blather, reporters are inclined to solemnly relay it—while adding some of their own.

The standard jargon of U.S. politics in the 1990s is the type of facile rhetoric that appalled Orwell. This lexicon derives its power from unexamined repetition.

To carry on Orwell's efforts, we should question the buzzwords that swarm all around us. For instance:

"Centrist"—A term of endearment in elite circles, usually affixed to politicians who don't rock boats, even ones stuck in stagnant waters.

"Reform"—This word once described change aimed at removing corruption or privilege. Now the word offers a favor-

able sheen to any policy shift. A linguistic loophole vague and gaping enough to drive a truck through, whatever the political cargo.

"Bipartisan"—An adjective that hails the two major parties for showing great unity and national purpose: usually agreed to behind closed doors, out of view of the riff-raff.

"Special interests"—A negative label commonly applied to mass constituencies of millions of people—seniors, the poor, racial minorities, union members, feminists, gays… Formerly a pejorative to describe monied interests that used dollars—since they lacked numbers of people—to influence politics.

"Sources say"—Leaks from on high, served up as journalistic champagne.

"Experts"—Oft-cited and carefully selected, they supply fertilizer for the next harvests of popular credulity.

"Defense budget"—Having precious little to do with actual defense of the country, these expenditures require the most innocent of names.

"Senior U.S. officials"—Unnamed, they are larger than life. In another culture they might be called "messengers of God."

"Rule of law"—What occurs when those who made the rules lay down the law—sometimes violently—overseas or at home.

"National security"—An ever-ready rationale for just about any diplomatic or military maneuver…or any suppression of incriminating information.

"Stability in the region"—Can be a tidy phrase to justify the continuation of existing horrors.

"*Western diplomats*"—These bastions of patience and wisdom provide the compass for navigating in foreign geopolitical waters.

"*The West*"—Often used as a synonym for global forces of good.

George Orwell wrote his last novel, *1984,* in the late 1940s—around the time the U.S. "War Department" became the "Defense Department." Orwell's novel anticipated that "the special function of certain Newspeak words" would be "not so much to express meanings as to destroy them."

The repetition of such words and phrases is never-ending. Like a constant drip on a stone, the cumulative effects are enormous.

Language, dialogue and debate are essential tools for a democratic process. But when words are wielded as blunt instruments, they bludgeon our minds rather than enhancing them.

The inflated shadow cast by words has grown in recent decades, but it is not new. "Identification of word with thing," Stuart Chase noted in 1938, "is well illustrated in the child's remark 'Pigs are rightly named, since they are such dirty animals.'"

Never better than imprecise symbols, words and phrases come to dominate the conceptual scenery—maps that are confused with the land itself. All too often, familiar words are used to label ideas and events instead of exploring them.

And over the years, evasive and euphemistic language— from "pacification programs" in Vietnam to "collateral damage" (killed civilians) in Iraq—has served as camouflage for inhuman policies.

George Orwell died young, succumbing to tuberculosis in 1950. But his acuity can be brought to life, to the extent that we probe beneath all the facile words and search out the realities they so often obscure.

June 23, 1993

The P.U.-litzer Prizes for 1993's Foulest Media Performances

It's that time again: Here are the second annual "P.U.-litzer Prizes"—highlighting some of the sorriest and smelliest media efforts of 1993.

News outlets love to crow when they or their employees win awards. But no one brags about winning a "P.U.-litzer." As always, the losers are us media consumers.

BEST KISS-UP INTERVIEW—John McLaughlin

On his show televised by the GE-owned cable network CNBC, a gushing John McLaughlin interviewed the co-author of *Control Your Destiny: How Jack Welch Is Making General Electric the World's Most Competitive Company*. McLaughlin and his guest invoked superlatives to describe the "brilliant" and "revolutionary" Welch, GE's top boss. McLaughlin didn't mention that Welch is the man behind GE's underwriting of the *McLaughlin Group* to the tune of $1 million per year.

"MY SOURCES SAY" AWARD—*Los Angeles Times*

Weeks after the World Trade Center bombing, Robin Wright's scary, front-page report in the *L.A. Times* warned that terrorism "will escalate against the United States and other countries." You can't blame Wright for the terror upsurge that didn't happen; she relied on the "experts." And who were they? We haven't a clue, since not one was named. The 22-paragraph story attributed facts, quotes, and "ominous assessments" 17 times to unnamed sources—"senior U.S. officials said"; "U.S. experts said"; "U.S. specialists say"; etc.

DUBIOUS SOURCE—*Washington Post*

A July 27 *Washington Post* article—headlined "Scientists Critique Media's Coverage of Cancer"—focused on a report that scolded news media for inflating "minor cancer risks." The

Post stated that the new report charged "the media overstate the cancer risks associated with nuclear power." What the *Post* didn't say is that the report's co-author, Mark Mills, has long been a paid consultant to the U.S. Council for Energy Awareness—the public relations arm of the nuclear industry.

MOST POORLY TIMED HATCHET-JOB—*New York Times* reporter Felicity Barringer

On March 6, Barringer's article in the *New York Times* implied that abortion rights groups—"like a conclave of unre-constructed Cold Warriors"—were exaggerating the threat of violence at family planning clinics. Four days later, Dr. David Gunn, a Florida physician who performed abortions, was murdered by an anti-abortion activist.

"WE MAKE THE RULES, WE BREAK THE RULES" AWARD—PBS

For years, PBS has used *conflict of interest* rules to reject programs about workers that were underwritten by unions...and to reject an Oscar-winning documentary about General Electric because the grass-roots group INFACT was both the funder and producer of the program. But in January, PBS bent its rules to broadcast a glowing documentary about *New York Times* columnist James Reston—which was funded by the *Times* and produced "in association with the *New York Times*" by a member of the family that owns the *Times*.

HALF-NAKED DOUBLE STANDARD AWARD—*Sports Illustrated*

The magazine that has cashed in on its annual swimsuit issue, featuring scantily clad women, refused to publish an ad because it showed partially naked men. In June, *Sports Illustrated* rejected an Adidas ad for its Canadian edition which featured a team of male soccer players, wearing only cleated shoes, covering their private parts with their hands or a ball or a trophy. "We just didn't feel it was appropriate," said a *Sports Illustrated* spokesman.

HAPPILY EVER NAFTA AWARD FOR BEST FAIRY TALE— Michael Kinsley of CNN's *Crossfire*

Debating a senator concerned about the flight of U.S. manufacturing jobs to Mexico, CNN's "leftist" Michael Kinsley argued vehemently in support of NAFTA: "What are these Mexicans going to do with these dollars they're earning? When these plants rush down to Mexico...and [the workers] earn dollars, those dollars are only good for one thing, which is buying stuff in the United States. You can't spend your dollars in Mexico. You can only spend them in the United States." Nice tale—except that Mexican workers are paid in pesos; and dollars are easily exchanged for pesos throughout Mexico, where goods are cheaper to buy.

HAPPILY EVER NAFTA AWARD II—Rush Limbaugh

"If you are unskilled and uneducated, your job is going south. Skilled workers, educated people are going to do fine 'cause those are the kinds of jobs NAFTA is going to create. If we are going to start rewarding no skills and stupid people, I'm serious, let the unskilled jobs that take absolutely no knowledge whatsoever to do—let stupid and unskilled Mexicans do that work."

"WE SPONSOR RACISTS AND SEXISTS FROM RIGHT TO 'LEFT'"—Snapple Beverage Corp.

In a letter answering a customer's complaint about its sponsorship of Rush Limbaugh, Snapple boasted of its commitment to diversity: "We do not necessarily agree with [Limbaugh's] point of view. For example, we are a sponsor of the Howard Stern radio and national television show. Howard Stern expresses opinions that are completely opposite to those of Rush Limbaugh. As a supporter of the right to freedom of speech, our advertising extends across all disciplines: from right to the left and everything in between."

BEST COLUMNIST OF THE (19TH) CENTURY—Patrick Buchanan

Furious that Carol Moseley-Braun had rallied her Senate colleagues to stop renewing the patent for a Confederate flag insignia, Buchanan rallied to the cause of the Confederacy: "The War Between the States was about independence, about self-determination, about the right of a people to break free of a government to which they could no longer give allegiance."

When Sen. Moseley-Braun associated the Confederacy with slavery, she was "putting on an act," according to Buchanan. "How long is this endless groveling before every cry of 'racism' going to continue before the whole country collectively throws up?"

There you have it: the P.U.-litzer Prizewinners for 1993. Hold your nose and get ready for '94.

December 22, 1993

Announcing the P.U.-litzer Prizes for 1994

Back by popular demand, here are the third annual P.U.-litzer Prizes—recognizing some of the stinkiest media performances of the year.

THE BEAUTIES OF BIAS AWARD—ABC's John Stossel

This fall, TV correspondent John Stossel acknowledged that he sees his job more as a promoter of "free-market" ideology than as a reporter. Known for ABC News specials and 20/20 segments deriding consumer protection and environmental regulations, Stossel told the *Oregonian* newspaper: "I started out by viewing the marketplace as a cruel place, where you need intervention by government and lawyers to protect people. But after watching the regulators work, I have come to believe that markets are magical and the best protectors of the consumer. It is my job to explain the beauties of the free market."

LOST IN SMOKE PRIZE—*Weekly Reader*

In October, sixth-graders read a *Weekly Reader* cover story reporting that "taxes and bans have caused many tobacco growers and workers to lose their jobs." Playing down the health effects of cigarettes, the article was illustrated by a photo of tobacco workers holding "No More Taxes" and "Freedom of Choice" placards. The 11-year-old readers weren't told that the rally pictured was organized by tobacco companies—nor that *Weekly Reader* is owned by a communications division of Kohlberg Kravis Roberts and Co., the largest investor in the RJR Nabisco tobacco firm.

MOST SIMPLEMINDED SCAPEGOATING—*Newsweek*'s Jonathan Alter

Competition in this category was fierce, with pundits frequently bashing low-income single mothers throughout the year. But *Newsweek* senior editor Jonathan Alter surged to a year-end victory with his Dec. 12 column, clinching the honor with a single sweeping sentence: "The fact remains: every threat to the fabric of this country—from poverty to crime to homelessness—is connected to out-of-wedlock teen pregnancy." *Every threat?* The export of manufacturing jobs to cheap-labor countries? Toxic pollution? Bigotry? The megabillion-dollar S&L rip-off?

MEDIA HYPOCRITE OF THE YEAR—Rupert Murdoch

Magnate Rupert Murdoch, owner of the Star TV global satellite network, has hailed the democratic power of new media technologies as a "threat to totalitarian regimes everywhere. Satellite broadcasting makes it possible for information-hungry residents of many closed societies to bypass state-controlled television." But to appease Chinese authorities—who were upset over Star TV's transmissions of BBC News reports on China's human rights abuses—Murdoch's network obligingly dropped the BBC from its broadcasts aimed at China. Too bad for "information-hungry residents."

DEMOCRATIC APARTHEID AWARD—*MacNeil/Lehrer NewsHour*

In a June 3 discussion about the effectiveness of economic sanctions...

Pundit Mark Shields: "The one place where there seems to be a success story and a lot of other factors converging on it for sanctions was South Africa."

Anchor Margaret Warner: "Where, of course, it was a democratic government."

Shields: "That's right."

So democratic that the vast majority of people couldn't vote.

THE OSCAR FOR CENSORSHIP GOES TO...—PBS, Lifetime Achievement

Year after year, Oscar-winning documentaries have been

declared unfit for national airing on PBS: For example, "The Panama Deception" about the U.S. invasion of Panama and "Deadly Deception" about General Electric's nuclear record. This year, no sooner had "Defending Our Lives" (about battered women) won an Oscar than PBS rejected it—on the grounds that the movie's co-producer was a leader of the battered women's group featured in the film.

PBS guidelines are remarkably flexible, however. Last year, PBS won a P.U.-litzer for airing a laudatory documentary about a *New York Times* columnist that was funded by the *Times* and produced "in association with the *New York Times.*"

DOWN THE MEMORY HOLE AWARD—*New York Times* and others

During a summer of historic anniversaries (the Moonwalk, Woodstock, Nixon's resignation, etc.) with profuse media reminiscences, major news outlets dodged the 30th anniversary of the fabricated Gulf of Tonkin crisis. The 1964 White House deception was swallowed by the national press, and ushered in the full-blown Vietnam War. In August 1994, on the very weekend of Tonkin's anniversary, the *New York Times* devoted a full-page spread to roughly three dozen anniversaries, including Chappaquiddick (25 years ago), Barbie dolls (35 years) and the bikini (50 years). No mention of Tonkin.

TWO-FACED TABLOID PRIZE—Ted Koppel

Although he has criticized the tabloidization of TV news, Ted Koppel began 1994 in the glitz lane with a focus on a story of global importance: the Tonya Harding/Nancy Kerrigan saga. In about seven weeks (Jan. 24 to March 16), *Nightline* devoted five entire broadcasts to the figure skaters—over 13 percent of total air time. During that period, *Nightline* offered no programs on such issues as unemployment, declining U.S. wages, world hunger or nuclear proliferation.

MAN OF THE PEOPLE PRIZE—Rush Limbaugh

On Jan. 28, Limbaugh told his TV audience: "All of these

rich guys—like the Kennedy family and Perot—pretending to live just like we do and pretending to understand our trials and tribulations and pretending to represent us, and they get away with this!" Limbaugh's income this year is estimated at $15 million.

Thankfully, that's all the prizes that space permits. Nominations for 1995 P.U.-litzers will soon be open. Please submit them in scented envelopes.

December 14, 1994

Index

Index